Confident Kids, Happy Kids: Parenting For Self-Esteem

Negoita Manuela

Published by Negoita Manuela, 2024.

While every precaution has been taken in the preparation of this book, the publisher assumes no responsibility for errors or omissions, or for damages resulting from the use of the information contained herein.

CONFIDENT KIDS, HAPPY KIDS: PARENTING FOR SELF-ESTEEM

First edition. March 30, 2024.

Copyright © 2024 Negoita Manuela.

ISBN: 979-8224881963

Written by Negoita Manuela.

Table of Contents

Chapter 1: Understanding Confidence

- What is confidence?

Confidence is a multifaceted concept that plays a crucial role in our daily lives, influencing how we navigate challenges, interact with others, and pursue our goals. At its core, confidence can be defined as a belief in oneself and one's abilities, a sense of self-assurance that empowers individuals to take risks, assert themselves, and face uncertainty with resilience. However, there are different dimensions to confidence that encompass various aspects of our psychosocial functioning, including self-esteem, self-efficacy, and self-perception. Understanding the nuances of confidence can provide valuable insights into how it develops, how it can be cultivated, and how it impacts our wellbeing and success.

Self-esteem is a fundamental component of confidence that involves an individual's overall evaluation of their self-worth and value. It is shaped by a multitude of factors, including early childhood experiences, social interactions, and personal achievements. People with high self-esteem tend to have a positive self-image, feel proud of themselves, and believe in their abilities to overcome obstacles. On the other hand, individuals with low self-esteem may struggle with feelings of inadequacy, self-doubt, and fear of failure. Building self-esteem requires self-awareness, self-acceptance, and self-compassion, as well as engaging in activities that promote personal growth and self-improvement.

Self-efficacy is another important aspect of confidence that pertains to a person's belief in their ability to succeed in specific tasks or situations. It is influenced by past experiences, feedback from others, and one's own perceptions of their skills and capabilities. Individuals with high self-efficacy are more likely to set challenging goals, persist in the face of setbacks, and view obstacles as opportunities for growth. By contrast, people with low self-efficacy may avoid challenges, doubt their abilities, and experience anxiety or self-doubt. Cultivating self-efficacy involves setting achievable goals, acquiring new skills, seeking support from others, and reframing negative thoughts or beliefs that undermine confidence.

Self-perception is a crucial aspect of confidence that encompasses how we view ourselves in relation to others and to the world around us. It includes our beliefs about our strengths and weaknesses, our values and goals, and our identity and self-concept. People with a positive self-perception tend to have a clear sense of who they are, what they stand for, and what they are capable of achieving. They are comfortable with themselves, feel secure in their relationships, and approach challenges with a sense of optimism and purpose. In contrast, individuals with a negative self-perception may struggle with self-doubt, insecurity, and a lack of direction or identity. Developing a positive self-perception involves cultivating self-awareness, self-acceptance, and self-compassion, as well as seeking validation and support from others who appreciate and value us for who we are.

Confidence is not a fixed or static trait but rather a dynamic and malleable quality that can be nurtured, strengthened, and developed over time. It is influenced by a complex interplay of internal and external factors, including genetics, upbringing, culture, and social influences. While some people may naturally possess a higher level of confidence than others, everyone has the capacity to enhance their confidence through intentional effort, practice, and self-reflection. Building confidence requires a willingness to step outside of one's comfort zone, confront fears and insecurities, and embrace challenges as opportunities for growth and learning. By cultivating self-esteem, self-efficacy, and self-perception, individuals can enhance their overall confidence and empower themselves to pursue their goals and dreams with assurance and resilience.

- The importance of confidence in children

Confidence plays a crucial role in the development and well-being of children. It is a key factor that influences their ability to navigate social situations, make decisions, and achieve their goals. As children grow and learn, having confidence in themselves and their abilities can have a significant impact on their overall success and happiness.

One of the main benefits of confidence in children is that it helps them to develop a positive self-image. When children believe in themselves and their abilities, they are more likely to have a strong sense of self-worth and value. This, in turn, can lead to greater resilience in the face of challenges and setbacks. Children who are confident are more likely to persevere in the face of obstacles, take risks, and push themselves to achieve their goals.

Confidence also plays a crucial role in children's social development. When children feel confident in themselves, they are more likely to interact with others in a positive and assertive manner. Confident children are more likely to speak up, express their thoughts and feelings, and assert their boundaries. This can help children to form healthy relationships with their peers and adults, as well as navigate conflicts and other social challenges.

Furthermore, confidence can also have a positive impact on children's academic performance. When children believe in their abilities, they are more likely to approach learning tasks with a positive attitude and a willingness to take on challenges. This can lead to greater engagement in the classroom, as well as improved academic outcomes. Confident children are more likely to ask questions, seek help when needed, and take risks in their learning, all of which can contribute to their academic success.

In addition to its impact on social and academic development, confidence in children can also have long-lasting effects on their mental health and well-being. Children who are confident are more likely to have a positive outlook on life, as well as greater emotional resilience. This can help them to cope with stress, anxiety, and other mental health challenges that may arise. Confidence can also act as a protective factor against things like bullying, peer pressure, and low self-esteem.

It is important to note that confidence is a skill that can be learned and developed over time. Parents, teachers, and other caregivers play a crucial role in helping children build and maintain confidence. By providing children with opportunities to try new things, make decisions, and take on challenges, adults can help to foster a sense of self-confidence in children. Encouraging children to take risks, problem-solve, and learn from their mistakes can also help to build their confidence. It can influence their self-image, social skills, academic performance, and mental health. By helping children to build and maintain confidence, adults can empower them to navigate the challenges of childhood and adolescence with resilience and strength. Confidence is a valuable skill that can benefit children throughout their lives, helping them to achieve their goals and lead fulfilling and successful lives.

- Factors that influence confidence development

Confidence development is a complex and multifaceted process that is influenced by a variety of factors. One of the key factors that can have a significant impact on an individual's confidence is their upbringing and early experiences. Children who are raised in environments where they are encouraged to take risks, explore new activities, and develop a sense of autonomy are more likely to grow up with a strong sense of self-confidence. On the other hand, children who are constantly criticized, micromanaged, or discouraged from trying new things may struggle to develop confidence in themselves and their abilities.

Another important factor that can influence confidence development is the individual's social environment. Friends, family members, teachers, and other significant people in a person's life can either bolster or undermine their confidence through their words and actions. Positive reinforcement, support, and encouragement from others can help boost an individual's confidence and belief in themselves. Conversely, negative feedback, criticism, and lack of support can have a detrimental effect on a person's confidence and self-esteem. It is important for individuals to surround themselves with people who uplift and empower them, rather than tear them down.

Self-perception and self-talk also play a crucial role in confidence development. The way we think about ourselves and the beliefs we hold about our abilities can either fuel our confidence or contribute to its decline. Positive self-talk, affirmations, and a growth mindset can help individuals build and maintain confidence in themselves. On the other hand, negative self-talk, self-doubt, and a fixed mindset can erode confidence and hold individuals back from reaching their full potential. It is important for individuals to work on cultivating a positive self-image and challenging negative thoughts and beliefs that may be hindering their confidence.

Personal experiences and achievements can also shape an individual's confidence levels. People who have a track record of success and accomplishments in various areas of their life are more likely to have a strong sense of self-confidence. On the other hand, repeated failures, setbacks, and disappointments can chip away at a person's confidence and belief in themselves. It is important for individuals to celebrate their successes, learn from their failures, and recognize their strengths and abilities in order to build and maintain confidence over time.

Lastly, societal and cultural norms can influence confidence development in individuals. Gender stereotypes, societal expectations, and cultural norms can impact how individuals view themselves and their capabilities. Women, for example, may face societal pressures to be modest, self-effacing, and accommodating, which can sometimes hinder their confidence and assertiveness. On the other hand, men may face expectations to be strong, independent, and unemotional, which can also impact their confidence and willingness to show vulnerability. It is important for individuals to challenge and deconstruct these societal and cultural norms in order to develop a healthy and balanced sense of confidence. From upbringing and early experiences to social environment, self-perception, personal achievements, and societal norms, there are many elements that play a role in shaping an individual's confidence levels. By understanding and addressing these factors, individuals can work towards building and maintaining a strong sense of self-confidence that empowers them to pursue their goals and dreams with courage and determination.

Chapter 2: Building Self-Esteem

- Difference between confidence and self-esteem

Confidence and self-esteem are two essential components of psychological well-being that are often misunderstood or conflated. While they both play a crucial role in how individuals perceive themselves and interact with the world around them, it is important to understand the distinct differences between the two concepts.

Confidence can be defined as the belief in one's ability to succeed or perform a specific task. It is a state of mind that allows individuals to trust in their skills, knowledge, and experience. Confidence is typically situation-specific, meaning that a person may feel confident in certain aspects of their life, such as public speaking or sports, while lacking confidence in other areas. Confidence is often built through repeated practice and positive reinforcement, as individuals gain a sense of competence and mastery in a particular domain.

On the other hand, self-esteem refers to a person's overall evaluation of their worth and value as a human being. It is a broader and more stable trait that encompasses how individuals view themselves in a global sense, regardless of their performance or achievements in specific areas. Self-esteem is influenced by various factors, such as upbringing, social relationships, and personal experiences, and can fluctuate over time. High self-esteem is associated with a positive self-image and a strong sense of self-worth, while low self-esteem can lead to feelings of inadequacy, self-doubt, and insecurity.

While confidence and self-esteem are related concepts, they are distinct in several key ways. Confidence is more focused on specific abilities and behaviors, such as public speaking or problem-solving, while self-esteem is a broader reflection of one's overall sense of self-worth and value. In other words, confidence is about believing in what you can do, while self-esteem is about believing in who you are as a person. Additionally, confidence tends to be more situation-specific and context-dependent, while self-esteem is a more stable and enduring trait that transcends specific circumstances.

It is important to note that confidence and self-esteem can influence each other in complex ways. For example, individuals with high self-esteem may be more likely to feel confident in their abilities and take on new challenges, while those with low self-esteem may struggle to believe in themselves even when they have the skills and knowledge to succeed. Similarly, building confidence in specific areas can help boost self-esteem by demonstrating to oneself that they are capable and competent in different domains.

There are also important implications for mental health and well-being when it comes to confidence and self-esteem. Research has shown that individuals with high levels of self-esteem are more resilient in the face of setbacks and challenges, as they have a strong internal foundation of self-worth to draw upon. On the other hand, low self-esteem has been linked to a range of mental health issues, such as depression, anxiety, and eating disorders, as individuals struggle to cope with negative self-perceptions and feelings of worthlessness. Confidence is about believing in one's abilities and skills in specific areas, while self-esteem is a broader reflection of one's overall sense of self-worth and value. Understanding the differences between confidence and self-esteem can help individuals cultivate both qualities in a balanced and healthy way, leading to greater mental well-being and fulfillment in life.

- Strategies for improving self-esteem in children

Self-esteem plays a critical role in a child's development and well-being. It is the foundation upon which they build their sense of self-worth, confidence, and resilience. Children with healthy self-esteem are more likely to excel academically, form positive relationships, and navigate life's challenges with ease. On the other hand, children with low self-esteem may struggle with feelings of inadequacy, self-doubt, and social anxiety. As a result, it is crucial for parents, educators, and caregivers to implement strategies that empower children to cultivate and maintain a positive self-image.

One of the most effective strategies for improving self-esteem in children is to provide them with unconditional love and support. Children need to know that they are valued and accepted for who they are, regardless of their accomplishments or failures. By creating a nurturing and safe environment, parents and caregivers can help children develop a sense of security and trust in themselves. This can be achieved through consistent praise, encouragement, and affection, as well as through active listening and empathy. When children feel loved and supported, they are more likely to believe in their abilities and worth.

In addition to providing emotional support, it is important for parents and caregivers to help children set realistic goals and expectations for themselves. Children often base their self-esteem on their perceived successes or failures, so it is crucial to help them develop a healthy sense of achievement. By setting achievable goals and celebrating small victories, children can build confidence and self-efficacy. It is important for adults to model a growth mindset and emphasize the importance of effort and perseverance over innate talent. By encouraging children to take risks, learn from their mistakes, and try new things, parents and caregivers can help them develop a sense of competence and mastery.

Furthermore, fostering a positive and nurturing relationship with children can also involve helping them develop their social skills and emotional intelligence. Children with strong interpersonal skills are better able to form meaningful relationships, communicate effectively, and resolve conflicts in a healthy manner. By teaching children how to empathize with others, express their feelings assertively, and make positive choices in their interactions, parents and caregivers can help them build strong and supportive social networks. This can help children feel more connected and accepted by their peers, further boosting their self-esteem and sense of belonging.

Another key strategy for improving self-esteem in children is to teach them effective coping strategies for managing stress, anxiety, and negative emotions. Children who are equipped with healthy coping mechanisms are better able to handle setbacks, disappointments, and challenges without becoming overwhelmed or discouraged. By teaching children relaxation techniques, such as deep breathing, mindfulness, or meditation, parents and caregivers can help them regulate their emotions and calm their minds during stressful situations. Additionally, helping children identify and challenge negative thought patterns, such as self-criticism or perfectionism, can empower them to cultivate a more positive and realistic self-image.

It is also important for parents and caregivers to promote a sense of autonomy and independence in children. By encouraging children to make choices, solve problems, and take responsibility for their actions, adults can help them develop a sense of agency and self-confidence. When children feel empowered to make decisions and assert their needs and desires, they are more likely to develop a strong sense of self-worth and self-efficacy. By providing children with opportunities to practice independence, such as through chores, homework, or extracurricular activities, parents and caregivers can help them develop important life skills and a sense of competence.

Moreover, it is crucial for parents and caregivers to be mindful of the language they use when interacting with children. Positive and affirming language can help children feel valued, respected, and capable. By avoiding harsh criticism, sarcasm, or negative labels, adults can help children develop a healthier self-image and sense of self-worth. It is important for adults to provide constructive feedback in a supportive and non-judgmental manner, focusing on the behavior or outcome rather than the child's character. By using encouraging words, such as "I believe in you" or "You can do it," parents and caregivers can instill confidence and motivation in children. By providing children with love, support, and encouragement, as well as teaching them important life skills and coping strategies, parents and caregivers can help them develop a positive self-image and sense of self-worth. By fostering a nurturing and empowering environment and modeling positive behaviors, adults can empower children to believe in themselves, overcome challenges, and succeed in life. Ultimately, by investing in children's self-esteem, we can help them build a strong foundation for a happy, healthy, and successful future.

- Encouraging positive self-talk

Positive self-talk is a powerful tool that can greatly impact our mental well-being and overall quality of life. It involves consciously changing the way we speak to ourselves in our minds, replacing negative thoughts and self-criticisms with positive affirmations and encouraging statements. By practicing positive self-talk regularly, we can improve our self-esteem, reduce stress and anxiety, and cultivate a more optimistic outlook on life. However, many people struggle to engage in positive self-talk consistently, either due to ingrained negative thought patterns or a lack of awareness of the benefits it can bring. In this essay, we will explore the importance of encouraging positive self-talk, discuss strategies for incorporating it into our daily lives, and examine the impact it can have on our mental and emotional well-being.

One of the key reasons why encouraging positive self-talk is so important is its impact on our self-esteem and self-confidence. When we constantly berate ourselves with negative thoughts and self-criticisms, we begin to internalize these beliefs and see ourselves in a negative light. This can lead to a downward spiral of low self-esteem, a lack of self-confidence, and a diminished sense of self-worth. On the other hand, by replacing these negative thoughts with positive affirmations and encouraging statements, we can start to see ourselves in a more positive and compassionate light. This can boost our self-esteem, increase our self-confidence, and ultimately improve our overall sense of self-worth. By practicing positive self-talk regularly, we can change the way we see ourselves and build a more positive self-image.

Another important reason to encourage positive self-talk is its ability to reduce stress and anxiety. Negative self-talk is often fueled by fear, anxiety, and self-doubt, which can create a cycle of negative emotions and thoughts. By practicing positive self-talk, we can interrupt this cycle and replace these negative thoughts with more positive and encouraging ones. This can help us to feel more in control of our thoughts and emotions, reduce our levels of stress and anxiety, and improve our overall well-being. By cultivating a more positive mindset through positive self-talk, we can increase our resilience to stress and anxiety and develop healthier coping mechanisms for dealing with life's challenges. Positive self-talk can be a valuable tool in managing stress and anxiety and improving our overall mental and emotional well-being.

In addition to its impact on self-esteem and stress, positive self-talk can also help us to cultivate a more optimistic outlook on life. When we engage in positive self-talk, we are consciously choosing to focus on the positive aspects of our lives and ourselves, rather than dwelling on the negative. This can help us to shift our perspective and see the world in a more hopeful and optimistic light. By practicing positive self-talk, we can train our minds to look for the good in every situation, see challenges as opportunities for growth, and approach life with a sense of optimism and possibility. This can lead to greater resilience, increased happiness, and a more positive overall outlook on life. By encouraging positive self-talk, we can cultivate a more optimistic mindset and create a more positive and fulfilling life for ourselves.

There are several strategies that we can use to encourage positive self-talk in our daily lives. One of the most effective strategies is to become more aware of our thoughts and catch ourselves when we engage in negative self-talk. By paying attention to the way we speak to ourselves in our minds, we can begin to identify the negative thought patterns that are holding us back and replace them with more positive affirmations. It can also be helpful to keep a journal of our thoughts and feelings, so we can track our progress and identify any recurring negative patterns that need to be addressed. By becoming more aware of our thoughts, we can start to challenge and change the negative beliefs that are holding us back and replace them with more positive and empowering affirmations.

Another effective strategy for encouraging positive self-talk is to practice self-compassion and treat ourselves with kindness and understanding. Often, we are our own harshest critics, constantly berating ourselves for perceived shortcomings or mistakes. By practicing self-compassion, we can learn to treat ourselves with the same kindness and understanding that we would offer to a friend in need. This can help us to challenge the negative self-talk that keeps us stuck in a cycle of self-doubt and self-criticism, and replace it with more positive and encouraging statements. By practicing self-compassion, we can cultivate a more gentle and loving relationship with ourselves, which can lead to increased self-esteem, reduced stress and anxiety, and a greater sense of well-being.

It can also be helpful to create a list of positive affirmations or encouraging statements that resonate with us and repeat them regularly throughout the day. By incorporating these affirmations into our daily routine, we can reinforce our commitment to positive self-talk and remind ourselves of our inherent worth and potential. These affirmations can be tailored to address specific areas of our lives where we struggle with negative self-talk, such as self-esteem, relationships, or career. By repeating these affirmations regularly, we can start to internalize these positive beliefs and create a more empowering and supportive inner dialogue. Positive affirmations can be a powerful tool for encouraging positive self-talk and cultivating a more positive mindset. By replacing negative thoughts and self-criticisms with positive affirmations and encouraging statements, we can boost our self-esteem, reduce stress and anxiety, and cultivate a more optimistic outlook on life. By becoming more aware of our thoughts, practicing self-compassion, and incorporating positive affirmations into our daily routine, we can start to shift our inner dialogue and create a more positive and empowering mindset. Positive self-talk is a powerful tool that can help us to see ourselves in a more positive light, build resilience to stress and adversity, and approach life with a greater sense of optimism and possibility. By encouraging positive self-talk, we can transform the way we see ourselves and the world around us, and create a more positive and fulfilling life for ourselves.

Chapter 3: Setting Realistic Expectations

- The role of expectations in building confidence

Confidence is a crucial aspect of success in both personal and professional spheres, and it is often influenced by a multitude of factors, one of which is expectations. Expectations play a significant role in shaping an individual's confidence levels, as they set the tone for how a person perceives their abilities and potential for success. When individuals have high expectations for themselves, they are more likely to have greater confidence in their abilities and be more motivated to achieve their goals.

Expectations can come from a variety of sources, including past experiences, societal norms, and personal beliefs. For example, if an individual has consistently received positive feedback in the past, they may have high expectations for future performance and be more confident in their abilities. On the other hand, if someone has faced criticism or failure in the past, they may have lower expectations for themselves and struggle with confidence issues. It is important for individuals to be aware of how their expectations can impact their confidence and take steps to manage and adjust them as needed.

One way in which expectations influence confidence is through the concept of self-fulfilling prophecies. This phenomenon occurs when individuals internalize and believe in their expectations, which then shape their behaviors and actions in a way that fulfills those expectations. For example, if someone expects to do well in a job interview, they may exude confidence, articulate their skills effectively, and ultimately perform well. Conversely, if someone goes into a situation with low expectations, they may be more hesitant, doubtful, and less likely to succeed.

It is important for individuals to be mindful of the impact that their expectations can have on their confidence levels and take steps to set realistic and achievable expectations. Setting high expectations for oneself can be motivating and empowering, but it is also important to strike a balance and not set unrealistic or unattainable goals. By setting goals that are challenging yet achievable, individuals can build confidence through a sense of accomplishment and success.

In addition to setting realistic expectations, individuals can also build confidence by seeking out support and feedback from others. Surrounding oneself with a supportive network of colleagues, mentors, and friends can provide valuable perspectives and encouragement that can help boost confidence levels. Constructive feedback can also be instrumental in helping individuals identify areas for improvement and grow in their confidence.

Furthermore, it is important for individuals to practice self-compassion and self-care in order to build and maintain confidence. Acknowledging and accepting one's strengths and weaknesses, while also taking care of their physical and emotional well-being, can help individuals feel more confident and resilient in the face of challenges. Engaging in activities that promote self-care, such as exercise, meditation, and spending time with loved ones, can help individuals cultivate a positive self-image and build confidence from within. By setting realistic and achievable expectations, seeking out support and feedback, and practicing self-compassion and self-care, individuals can strengthen their confidence levels and achieve greater success in their personal and professional lives. By being mindful of the impact of expectations and taking proactive steps to manage and adjust them as needed, individuals can cultivate a strong sense of self-assurance and belief in their abilities.

- Understanding the concept of perfectionism

Perfectionism is a pervasive and often misunderstood concept that can have significant impacts on an individual's well-being and success. In its simplest form, perfectionism can be described as the relentless pursuit of flawlessness, coupled with critical self-evaluations and a fear of making mistakes. However, there are different dimensions of perfectionism that can manifest in various ways in individuals.

One common misconception about perfectionism is that it is synonymous with high achievement or excellence. While perfectionists may indeed achieve great success in their endeavors, their motivation is often driven by a deep-seated fear of failure rather than a genuine passion for the task at hand. This fear can lead to a constant state of anxiety and stress, as perfectionists strive to meet impossibly high standards and are never satisfied with their own performance.

Perfectionism can also have negative effects on relationships and mental health. Perfectionists tend to be highly critical of themselves and others, which can create friction in personal and professional relationships. Additionally, the constant pressure to be flawless can lead to feelings of inadequacy, depression, and burnout. Perfectionists may also struggle to delegate tasks or seek help from others, as they believe that only they can meet their exacting standards.

It is important to recognize that perfectionism is not inherently a character flaw or personality trait, but rather a coping mechanism that is often rooted in childhood experiences or societal pressures. For example, individuals who grew up in environments where their worth was tied to their achievements may develop perfectionistic tendencies as a way to garner approval and acceptance from others. Similarly, societal messages that equate success with perfection can fuel perfectionistic tendencies in individuals.

In order to address perfectionism, it is crucial to first recognize and acknowledge its presence in one's life. This may involve reflecting on past experiences and recognizing patterns of behavior that are driven by perfectionistic tendencies. It is also important to challenge the beliefs and expectations that underpin perfectionism, such as the idea that mistakes are intolerable or that self-worth is contingent on flawless performance.

Once the presence of perfectionism is acknowledged, individuals can begin to cultivate self-compassion and self-acceptance. This may involve reframing unrealistic expectations, setting more realistic goals, and embracing imperfection as a natural part of the human experience. Developing a growth mindset, which emphasizes learning and growth rather than perfection, can also help individuals shift their perspective and foster a healthier relationship with themselves and their goals.

Therapy or counseling can also be helpful for individuals struggling with perfectionism. Cognitive-behavioral therapy (CBT) and acceptance and commitment therapy (ACT) are two approaches that have been found to be effective in helping individuals challenge perfectionistic beliefs and develop more adaptive coping strategies. In therapy, individuals can explore the underlying causes of their perfectionism, develop healthy ways of responding to failure and setbacks, and learn to cultivate self-compassion and acceptance. By recognizing and challenging perfectionistic tendencies, individuals can begin to cultivate self-compassion, set more realistic goals, and develop healthier ways of coping with stress and failure. Therapy can also be a helpful tool in addressing perfectionism and developing more adaptive coping strategies. Ultimately, by embracing imperfection and valuing growth over flawlessness, individuals can create a more balanced and fulfilling life for themselves.

- Strategies for setting realistic goals

Setting realistic goals is an essential component of achieving success in any aspect of life. Whether it be personal, professional, or academic goals, having a clear understanding of what you want to accomplish and how you plan to achieve it is crucial. In this article, we will discuss some strategies for setting realistic goals that are both achievable and meaningful. By following these strategies, you can increase your chances of success and make steady progress towards your desired outcomes.

One of the first steps in setting realistic goals is to clearly define what it is that you want to achieve. This involves taking the time to reflect on your values, interests, and passions, and considering what truly matters to you. By identifying your core values and priorities, you can set goals that are aligned with your true desires and motivations. This will help to keep you focused and motivated as you work towards achieving your goals.

Once you have a clear understanding of what you want to achieve, it is important to break down your goals into smaller, more manageable tasks. Setting smaller, achievable milestones along the way can help to keep you motivated and on track towards your ultimate goal. By breaking down your larger goal into smaller steps, you can also more easily track your progress and make adjustments as needed. This can help to prevent feelings of overwhelm and ensure that you are making steady progress towards your desired outcome.

Another important strategy for setting realistic goals is to be specific and concrete in your goal-setting. Vague or ambiguous goals can be difficult to measure and track, making it harder to gauge your progress and make adjustments as needed. Instead, aim to set goals that are clear, specific, and measurable. For example, rather than setting a goal to "lose weight," you could set a goal to "lose 10 pounds in the next three months. " This gives you a specific target to aim for and a clear timeline for achieving it.

In addition to being specific and concrete, it is also important to set goals that are realistic and achievable. While it is important to challenge yourself and set goals that push you outside of your comfort zone, it is also important to be realistic about what you can accomplish within a given timeframe. Setting goals that are too ambitious or unrealistic can lead to feelings of failure and discouragement, which can ultimately prevent you from achieving your desired outcomes. Instead, aim to set goals that are challenging yet attainable, taking into account your current abilities, resources, and constraints.

A key aspect of setting realistic goals is to ensure that they are relevant and meaningful to you. Goals that are not personally meaningful are less likely to be achieved, as you may lack the motivation and commitment needed to pursue them. Before setting a goal, take the time to consider why it is important to you and how achieving it will impact your life. By setting goals that are aligned with your values, passions, and aspirations, you are more likely to stay motivated and committed to achieving them.

In addition to setting specific, measurable, achievable, and relevant goals, it is also important to set goals that are time-bound. Setting a clear deadline for achieving your goals can help to keep you focused and motivated, and provide a sense of urgency to your actions. Without a deadline, you may be more likely to procrastinate or lose momentum towards your goals. By setting a timeline for achieving your goals, you can more effectively track your progress and make adjustments as needed to stay on track.

In ending, it is important to regularly review and reassess your goals to ensure that they are still relevant and aligned with your current priorities and values. As you progress towards achieving your goals, you may find that your circumstances change or that new opportunities arise that require you to adjust your goals. By regularly reviewing and reassessing your goals, you can ensure that they remain meaningful and relevant to you, and make any necessary adjustments to keep you on track towards your desired outcomes. By following the strategies outlined in this article - including defining your goals, breaking them down into smaller tasks, being specific and concrete, setting realistic and achievable goals, ensuring that they are relevant and meaningful, setting deadlines, and regularly reviewing and reassessing your goals - you can increase your chances of success and make steady progress towards your desired outcomes. By setting realistic goals and taking consistent action towards achieving them, you can make your dreams a reality and create the life you desire.

Chapter 4: Positive Reinforcement

- The power of positive reinforcement

Positive reinforcement is a powerful tool that can be used to influence behavior in both individuals and organizations. By providing positive feedback or rewards for desired actions, positive reinforcement can strengthen and increase the likelihood of those behaviors being repeated in the future. This principle, often associated with the work of behaviorist B. F. Skinner, has been widely studied and applied in various fields, including psychology, education, and business management. In this essay, we will explore the concept of positive reinforcement in more detail, discussing its effectiveness, benefits, and practical applications.

One of the key benefits of positive reinforcement is its ability to enhance motivation and performance. When individuals receive positive feedback or rewards for their efforts, they are more likely to feel encouraged and motivated to continue putting in their best work. This can lead to increased productivity, better results, and a more positive work environment. In educational settings, positive reinforcement has been shown to improve student engagement and academic performance. By acknowledging and rewarding students for their achievements, teachers can create a supportive and empowering learning environment that fosters success.

Another important aspect of positive reinforcement is its role in shaping behavior. By associating specific behaviors with positive outcomes, individuals are more likely to engage in those behaviors in the future. This can be particularly useful in the workplace, where managers can use positive reinforcement to encourage desired behaviors, such as meeting deadlines, collaborating with colleagues, or providing excellent customer service. By recognizing and rewarding employees for their efforts, managers can create a culture of excellence and accountability that drives performance and success.

Positive reinforcement is also valuable in building relationships and fostering a positive culture within organizations. When individuals feel appreciated and valued for their contributions, they are more likely to develop strong connections with their peers and superiors. This can lead to improved communication, collaboration, and teamwork, which are essential for organizational success. By using positive reinforcement to reinforce desired behaviors and values, leaders can create a culture of trust, respect, and positivity that motivates employees to excel and achieve their goals. By acknowledging and rewarding individuals for their efforts and achievements, leaders can create an empowering and supportive environment that drives performance and success. Whether applied in educational settings, business management, or personal relationships, positive reinforcement has the potential to inspire greatness and bring out the best in people. As we continue to explore and leverage the power of positive reinforcement, we can create a world where individuals are motivated, engaged, and empowered to achieve their full potential.

- Effective ways to praise children

Praising children is an essential aspect of their emotional and cognitive development. When done effectively, praise can boost a child's self-esteem, increase their motivation, and encourage positive behavior. However, it is important to praise children in a way that is meaningful and genuine, as empty or insincere praise can have negative effects on a child's self-esteem and motivation. In this paper, we will explore some effective ways to praise children in order to help them thrive and succeed.

One effective way to praise children is to be specific and descriptive in your feedback. Instead of simply saying "good job," try to specifically mention what the child did well and why it was successful. For example, instead of saying "good job on your art project," you could say "I love the way you used different colors and shapes in your art project. It shows how creative you are and how much effort you put into it. " This type of specific and descriptive feedback helps children understand what they did well and encourages them to continue improving in that area.

Another effective way to praise children is to focus on their effort and progress, rather than just their achievements. This type of praise helps children develop a growth mindset, where they believe that their abilities can be developed through hard work and perseverance. Instead of praising a child for getting an A on a test, you could praise them for how hard they studied and how much progress they have made since the last test. This type of praise reinforces the idea that success comes from effort and perseverance, rather than innate ability.

It is also important to praise children for their character traits and values, rather than just their actions or achievements. By praising children for qualities such as kindness, empathy, and resilience, you help them develop a strong sense of self-worth and identity. For example, instead of praising a child for winning a game, you could praise them for being a good sport and showing kindness to their teammates, win or lose. This type of praise reinforces the importance of character traits and values, and encourages children to prioritize these qualities in their actions and decisions.

In addition to being specific, focusing on effort and progress, and praising character traits and values, it is also important to consider the timing and delivery of praise. Praise should be given immediately after the desired behavior or action, in order to reinforce the connection between the behavior and the praise. For example, if a child shares a toy with a friend, you should praise them right away by saying something like "I really appreciate how you shared your toy with your friend. That was very kind of you. " This immediate feedback helps children understand which behaviors are valued and encourages them to continue behaving in that way.

Furthermore, it is important to vary the types of praise you give to children. While verbal praise is important and effective, other forms of praise, such as tangible rewards or gestures of appreciation, can also be beneficial. For example, you could create a reward chart for a child who is working on a specific goal, and provide stickers or small prizes as a way to recognize their progress and effort. These additional forms of praise can help keep children motivated and engaged, and reinforce the positive behaviors you are trying to encourage. By being specific and descriptive, focusing on effort and progress, praising character traits and values, considering the timing and delivery of praise, and varying the types of praise given, parents and educators can help children thrive and succeed. When done consistently and genuinely, praise can help build children's self-esteem, motivation, and resilience, and set them on a path towards a successful and fulfilling future.

- Recognizing and celebrating achievements

Recognizing and celebrating achievements is an essential aspect of human existence that helps to motivate individuals and inspire others to reach their full potential. It is important to acknowledge the hard work, dedication, and accomplishments of individuals to promote a culture of excellence and encourage continuous improvement. Whether it is in the academic, professional, or personal spheres of life, recognition and celebration of achievements play a significant role in shaping individuals' self-esteem, confidence, and overall well-being.

In the academic realm, recognizing and celebrating achievements is crucial for fostering a positive learning environment and encouraging students to strive for excellence. When students receive recognition for their academic accomplishments, such as high grades, exceptional performance in extracurricular activities, or academic awards, they are more likely to be motivated to continue working hard and pursuing their academic goals. Recognizing and celebrating achievements also help to build a sense of community within educational institutions, as students, teachers, and parents come together to celebrate the success of students and acknowledge their efforts and dedication.

In the professional world, recognition and celebration of achievements are equally important for boosting employee morale, fostering a positive work culture, and increasing productivity. When employees are recognized and rewarded for their hard work, dedication, and achievements, they are more likely to feel valued, appreciated, and motivated to perform at their best. Recognizing and celebrating achievements in the workplace also help to create a sense of camaraderie among employees, as they come together to celebrate each other's successes and support each other in their professional development.

On a personal level, recognizing and celebrating achievements can have a profound impact on an individual's self-esteem, confidence, and overall well-being. Whether it is achieving a personal goal, overcoming a challenge, or making a positive impact in the community, celebrating achievements can help individuals feel a sense of pride, satisfaction, and fulfillment. Recognizing and celebrating achievements can also serve as a source of motivation and inspiration for others, as they see the success and accomplishments of those around them and are encouraged to set their own goals and strive to achieve them. Whether it is in the academic, professional, or personal spheres, recognizing and celebrating achievements helps to build a culture of excellence, foster a sense of community, boost morale and productivity, and promote overall well-being. By acknowledging the hard work, dedication, and accomplishments of individuals, we can create a positive and supportive environment that encourages individuals to reach their full potential and celebrate their successes.

Chapter 5: Resilience and Coping Skills

- Teaching children how to bounce back from failure

When it comes to teaching children how to bounce back from failure, it is important to emphasize the value of resilience and the ability to overcome challenges. Failure is a natural part of life and can provide valuable learning opportunities for children. By teaching children how to view failure as a stepping stone to success rather than a roadblock, we can help them develop the resilience and skills needed to navigate life's ups and downs.

One key aspect of teaching children how to bounce back from failure is to encourage a growth mindset. This means teaching children that their abilities are not fixed, but can be developed through effort and perseverance. By instilling a growth mindset in children, we can help them approach failure with a sense of optimism and a willingness to keep trying until they succeed. This can help children develop a sense of resilience and self-efficacy that will serve them well in the face of future challenges.

Another important aspect of teaching children how to bounce back from failure is to provide them with opportunities to practice resilience in a safe and supportive environment. This can involve setting up activities that challenge children to try new things and overcome obstacles, while also providing them with the support and guidance they need to navigate these challenges successfully. By gradually increasing the level of difficulty and complexity of these activities, we can help children build their resilience and confidence over time.

It is also important to teach children the value of self-reflection and learning from failure. By encouraging children to reflect on their experiences and identify what they have learned from their failures, we can help them develop a sense of self-awareness and growth. This can help children understand that failure is not a reflection of their worth or abilities, but rather an opportunity to learn and grow. By helping children develop a positive attitude towards failure, we can empower them to bounce back stronger and more resilient than before.

In addition to teaching children how to bounce back from failure, it is important to provide them with support and encouragement along the way. This can involve offering praise and recognition for their efforts, as well as providing them with constructive feedback and guidance to help them improve. By creating a supportive and nurturing environment, we can help children feel safe and secure as they navigate the challenges of failure. This can help children develop a sense of trust and confidence in their abilities, which can in turn help them bounce back from failure more effectively. By emphasizing the value of resilience, instilling a growth mindset, providing opportunities for practice, encouraging self-reflection, and offering support and encouragement, we can help children develop the skills and attitudes they need to bounce back from failure and thrive in the face of adversity. By teaching children how to view failure as a natural part of the learning process, we can empower them to face life's challenges with a sense of optimism and determination.

- Tools for developing coping skills

Developing coping skills is essential for managing stress and navigating through life's challenges. Coping skills are the strategies individuals use to handle difficult situations, emotions, and thoughts in a healthy and adaptive way. These skills help us to effectively deal with stressors, reduce negative emotions, and maintain overall mental well-being. While everyone has their own unique coping mechanisms, there are several tools and techniques that can help individuals develop and strengthen their coping skills.

One of the most effective tools for developing coping skills is mindfulness. Mindfulness is the practice of being fully present and aware in the moment, without judgment or distraction. By focusing on the present moment, individuals can better manage their emotions, reduce stress, and improve their overall well-being. Mindfulness techniques such as deep breathing, meditation, and body scan exercises can help individuals stay grounded and centered during challenging times. By incorporating mindfulness into their daily routine, individuals can develop a greater sense of self-awareness and resilience.

Another tool for developing coping skills is cognitive-behavioral therapy (CBT). CBT is a type of therapy that focuses on changing negative thought patterns and behaviors that contribute to stress and anxiety. By identifying and challenging distorted thinking patterns, individuals can learn to reframe their thoughts in a more positive and realistic way. CBT also teaches individuals practical coping skills, such as problem-solving strategies, relaxation techniques, and assertiveness training. By learning these skills, individuals can better manage their emotions and cope with stress in a healthier way.

Physical exercise is another important tool for developing coping skills. Exercise has been shown to reduce stress, improve mood, and increase overall well-being. By engaging in regular physical activity, individuals can release built-up tension and boost their endorphin levels, which are natural mood boosters. Whether it's going for a run, taking a yoga class, or going for a swim, finding an exercise routine that works for you can be a powerful way to manage stress and enhance resilience. Exercise can also help individuals develop a sense of accomplishment and self-confidence, which can improve coping skills in the long run.

Social support is another crucial tool for developing coping skills. Having a strong support network of friends, family, and peers can provide individuals with emotional validation, guidance, and encouragement during difficult times. By sharing their thoughts and feelings with others, individuals can gain new perspectives, receive advice, and feel less alone in their struggles. Social support can also help individuals build resilience and develop coping skills by providing a sense of belonging and connection. Whether it's joining a support group, talking to a trusted friend, or seeking guidance from a therapist, reaching out to others can be a powerful way to enhance coping skills.

In addition to these tools, practicing self-care is essential for developing coping skills. Self-care involves taking care of one's physical, emotional, and mental well-being through activities that promote relaxation, joy, and rejuvenation.

Whether it's taking a warm bath, reading a book, or going for a walk in nature, finding activities that nurture and replenish you can help you recharge and cope with stress more effectively. Self-care also involves setting boundaries, prioritizing your needs, and practicing self-compassion. By making self-care a priority in your daily routine, you can enhance your coping skills and improve your overall well-being. By incorporating tools such as mindfulness, cognitive-behavioral therapy, physical exercise, social support, and self-care into your daily routine, you can strengthen your coping skills and navigate through life's challenges in a healthy and adaptive way. Remember that coping skills are not static – they can be developed and strengthened over time through practice and persistence. By prioritizing your mental health and well-being, you can become better equipped to handle whatever life throws at you.

- Encouraging a growth mindset

Encouraging a growth mindset is an essential aspect of personal and academic development. A growth mindset is the belief that intelligence and abilities can be developed through hard work, dedication, and perseverance. Individuals with a growth mindset are more likely to embrace challenges, show resilience in the face of setbacks, and view failure as an opportunity for growth and learning. In contrast, individuals with a fixed mindset believe that intelligence and abilities are static traits that cannot be changed, leading to a fear of failure and a reluctance to take on new challenges.

One key way to encourage a growth mindset is through praising effort and persistence rather than innate talent or intelligence. When individuals receive praise for their hard work and perseverance, they are more likely to believe that these qualities are important for success. This can help foster a sense of resilience and a willingness to take on new challenges, knowing that their efforts will be recognized and valued. In contrast, praising innate talent or intelligence can reinforce a fixed mindset, leading individuals to believe that success is determined by factors beyond their control.

Another important way to promote a growth mindset is through providing opportunities for reflection and feedback. Encouraging individuals to reflect on their progress, identify areas for improvement, and seek feedback from others can help them develop a greater sense of self-awareness and a willingness to learn from their mistakes. By providing constructive feedback and guidance, educators and mentors can help individuals see failure as a natural part of the learning process and an opportunity for growth and improvement.

Creating a supportive and inclusive learning environment is also crucial for encouraging a growth mindset. When individuals feel safe and supported, they are more likely to take risks, try new things, and push themselves outside of their comfort zones. By fostering a sense of belonging and community, educators can help individuals develop the confidence and resilience needed to embrace challenges and overcome setbacks. This can help create a culture of continuous learning and improvement, where individuals are encouraged to push themselves beyond their limits and strive for excellence.

In addition to these strategies, it is important to recognize the role that mindset plays in shaping our beliefs and behaviors. By understanding the power of mindset, individuals can learn to challenge their self-limiting beliefs and adopt a more growth-oriented perspective. This can help individuals develop the resilience, grit, and determination needed to navigate the complexities of life and achieve their full potential. By encouraging a growth mindset in ourselves and others, we can create a more positive and empowering learning environment that fosters personal and academic growth.

Chapter 6: Embracing Individuality

- Celebrating diversity and uniqueness

Diversity and uniqueness are two essential elements that contribute to the richness and vibrancy of the human experience. They encompass a wide range of characteristics, including but not limited to race, ethnicity, culture, gender, sexual orientation, age, disability, and socioeconomic status. Celebrating diversity and uniqueness involves recognizing and valuing the differences that exist among individuals and communities, as well as appreciating the various perspectives and experiences they bring to the table.

One of the key reasons why celebrating diversity and uniqueness is important is because it promotes inclusivity and equality in society. By acknowledging and embracing the differences that make each of us unique, we create a more inclusive environment where everyone feels valued and respected. This, in turn, helps foster a sense of belonging and acceptance, which is essential for building strong and cohesive communities.

Furthermore, celebrating diversity and uniqueness also helps challenge stereotypes and prejudices that often perpetuate discrimination and inequality. When we take the time to learn about and understand the experiences and perspectives of others who may be different from us, we are better able to combat harmful stereotypes and prejudices that can lead to discrimination and oppression. By celebrating diversity and uniqueness, we can promote a more compassionate and empathetic society that values and respects individuals for who they are.

In addition, celebrating diversity and uniqueness can also lead to increased creativity and innovation. When individuals from diverse backgrounds come together, they bring with them a wealth of different perspectives, ideas, and experiences that can enrich the creative process and lead to new and innovative solutions to complex problems. Research has shown that diverse teams are often more creative and successful in their endeavors because they are able to draw on a wider range of skills and talents that can lead to more dynamic and innovative outcomes.

Moreover, celebrating diversity and uniqueness helps promote a sense of pride and identity in individuals and communities. When individuals are able to express and celebrate their unique identities, cultures, and backgrounds, they develop a sense of pride and self-confidence that can help them navigate the challenges and obstacles they may face in their lives. By celebrating diversity and uniqueness, we empower individuals to embrace who they are and take pride in their identities, thereby fostering a strong sense of self-worth and confidence. By recognizing and valuing the differences that exist among us, we can foster a sense of belonging and acceptance that promotes equality and mutual respect. Through celebrating diversity and uniqueness, we can challenge stereotypes and prejudices, promote creativity and innovation, and empower individuals to embrace their unique identities and experiences. In doing so, we can build stronger, more cohesive communities that value and respect the diverse range of perspectives and experiences that make each of us unique.

- Helping children embrace their differences

Children are unique individuals with their own set of characteristics, preferences, and abilities. It is important for parents, teachers, and society as a whole to help children embrace their differences and celebrate what makes them special. By promoting acceptance and understanding of diversity, we can create a more inclusive and supportive environment for all children to thrive.

One way to help children embrace their differences is to encourage open and honest conversations about diversity. This can be done through books, movies, and other media that showcase people of different backgrounds, cultures, and abilities. By exposing children to a variety of perspectives, they can learn to appreciate the richness and beauty of diversity. Teachers can also incorporate lessons on acceptance and empathy into their curriculum, fostering a sense of understanding and respect for all individuals.

Another important aspect of helping children embrace their differences is to model positive behavior and attitudes. Children are incredibly observant and learn through imitation. By demonstrating acceptance, kindness, and inclusivity in our own actions and words, we can set a powerful example for children to follow. This can include actively seeking out diverse friendships and experiences, standing up against discrimination and prejudice, and promoting a sense of belonging for all children.

It is also crucial to provide children with the tools and resources they need to navigate and embrace their differences. This can include access to mental health services, support groups, and education on self-acceptance and self-esteem. By equipping children with the skills and confidence to embrace their differences, we can empower them to overcome challenges and thrive in a world that may not always be accepting or understanding.

Additionally, it is important to create a safe and supportive environment for children to express themselves and explore their identities. This can involve creating safe spaces in schools and communities where children can be themselves without fear of judgment or discrimination. It can also involve promoting policies and practices that protect the rights and dignity of all individuals, regardless of their differences. By promoting acceptance, understanding, and celebration of diversity, we can create a world where all children feel valued, supported, and empowered to be their authentic selves. It is up to all of us to cultivate a culture of acceptance and inclusivity, one child at a time.

- Respecting and valuing others' uniqueness

Respecting and valuing others' uniqueness is a crucial aspect of building strong relationships and promoting a positive work environment. When we acknowledge and appreciate the individual differences that make each person unique, we create a culture of inclusivity and mutual respect. This not only fosters a sense of belonging and acceptance but also promotes creativity and innovation. By recognizing that each person has their own strengths, perspectives, and experiences to bring to the table, we can leverage these differences to drive collaboration and success.

One of the key principles of respecting and valuing others' uniqueness is recognizing that diversity enriches our lives and perspectives. Each person has a unique set of skills, talents, and experiences that contribute to the collective knowledge and capabilities of a team. By embracing these differences, we can harness the power of diversity to solve complex problems, generate new ideas, and drive innovation. When we value others' uniqueness, we are better able to tap into their potential and create an environment where everyone can thrive and succeed.

Another important aspect of respecting and valuing others' uniqueness is practicing empathy and understanding. By taking the time to listen to others, show empathy, and seek to understand their perspectives, we can build stronger relationships and cultivate a culture of trust and respect. When we approach interactions with an open mind and a willingness to learn from others, we not only demonstrate respect for their uniqueness but also create a space where people feel valued and understood. This can lead to improved communication, collaboration, and teamwork, ultimately driving better outcomes for individuals and organizations.

In addition to empathy and understanding, it is also crucial to recognize and celebrate the differences that make each person unique. Whether it be differences in culture, background, beliefs, or personality, each individual brings a valuable perspective to the table that should be acknowledged and appreciated. By celebrating diversity and promoting inclusivity, we can create a more welcoming and supportive environment where all individuals feel accepted and valued for who they are. This can lead to increased morale, engagement, and productivity, as well as a more positive and harmonious workplace culture.

Furthermore, respecting and valuing others' uniqueness can also help to prevent bias and discrimination in the workplace. By embracing diversity and actively promoting inclusivity, we can challenge stereotypes, prejudices, and biases that may exist within our organizations. By valuing others for their unique qualities and treating everyone with dignity and respect, we can create a culture that is free from discrimination and bias. This can lead to a more equitable and just workplace where all individuals have equal opportunities to succeed and thrive. By recognizing and appreciating the individual differences that make each person unique, we can create a culture of respect, empathy, and understanding. This can lead to improved collaboration, communication, and teamwork, as well as increased creativity, innovation, and success. By embracing diversity and celebrating the differences that make us unique, we can create a more inclusive, equitable, and supportive environment where all individuals feel valued and respected for who they are.

Chapter 7: Healthy Communication

- The importance of open and honest communication

Open and honest communication is a crucial element in any successful relationship, whether it be personal or professional. It is the foundation upon which trust, understanding, and respect are built. Without open and honest communication, misunderstandings can arise, leading to conflict, resentment, and ultimately, the breakdown of the relationship. Therefore, it is essential to prioritize clear and transparent communication in all interactions.

In the workplace, open and honest communication is vital for a harmonious and productive environment. When employees feel free to express their thoughts, ideas, and concerns without fear of reprisal, they are more likely to be engaged, motivated, and committed to their work. Furthermore, open communication allows for the sharing of information, feedback, and goals, leading to better collaboration and teamwork.

In personal relationships, open and honest communication is equally important. When partners are able to communicate openly and honestly with each other, they can build a stronger emotional connection and deeper intimacy. By sharing their thoughts, feelings, and needs with each other, they can better understand each other's perspectives and work together to address any issues or challenges they may face. This can lead to a more fulfilling and satisfying relationship built on trust, respect, and mutual support.

One of the key benefits of open and honest communication is the fostering of trust. When individuals are able to speak freely and honestly with each other, they are more likely to believe that the other person has their best interests at heart. This can create a sense of safety and security within the relationship, allowing both parties to be vulnerable and authentic with each other. Trust is essential for building strong relationships, and open communication is a powerful way to establish and maintain it.

Another important aspect of open and honest communication is the ability to resolve conflicts effectively. Conflicts are a natural part of any relationship, but how they are handled can make all the difference. By communicating openly and honestly with each other, individuals can express their thoughts and feelings in a constructive manner, listen to each other's perspectives, and work together to find a resolution that is mutually beneficial. This can help to prevent conflicts from escalating and damaging the relationship, and instead, foster understanding, empathy, and compromise.

In addition to building trust and resolving conflicts, open and honest communication also plays a crucial role in creating a positive and supportive environment. When individuals feel comfortable expressing themselves and being heard, they are more likely to feel valued, respected, and appreciated. This can lead to increased morale, motivation, and job satisfaction in the workplace, as well as greater emotional connection and intimacy in personal relationships. Therefore, it is important to prioritize open and honest communication in all interactions, as it is the key to building strong and lasting relationships based on trust, respect, and understanding.

- Building strong parent-child relationships

Research has consistently shown that positive parent-child relationships can have a significant impact on a child's emotional, social, and cognitive development. When children feel loved, supported, and understood by their parents, they are more likely to thrive and succeed in various aspects of their lives.

One of the key elements of building a strong parent-child relationship is communication. Effective communication involves not only talking to your child, but also actively listening to what they have to say. It is important for parents to create an open and safe space where their child feels comfortable expressing their thoughts, feelings, and concerns. By listening attentively and responding with empathy and understanding, parents can demonstrate to their child that their feelings and opinions are valued.

Another important aspect of building strong parent-child relationships is spending quality time together. Quality time does not necessarily have to be extravagant or planned activities; it can be as simple as reading a book together, going for a walk, or having a family dinner. The key is to be present and engaged during these moments, and to show your child that they are a priority in your life. By spending quality time together, parents can foster a sense of connection and intimacy with their child, which can strengthen their bond.

Furthermore, consistency and reliability are essential in building strong parent-child relationships. Children thrive on routine and predictability, and knowing that their parents are there for them consistently can provide a sense of stability and security. By setting clear expectations and boundaries, and following through on them, parents can build trust and reliability with their child.

It is also important for parents to show love and affection towards their child in a variety of ways. Physical touch, such as hugs and kisses, can communicate love and warmth to a child. Verbal expressions of affection, such as saying "I love you" or giving compliments, can also make a child feel valued and appreciated. Showing love and affection towards your child on a regular basis can help strengthen the emotional bond between parent and child, and can contribute to a positive parent-child relationship.

In addition to these strategies, it is important for parents to be understanding and supportive of their child's emotions and needs. Children may experience a wide range of emotions, from joy and excitement to frustration and sadness, and it is important for parents to validate and acknowledge these feelings. By providing a safe and supportive environment for their child to express their emotions, parents can help their child develop emotional intelligence and coping skills. Being empathetic and understanding towards their child can help strengthen the parent-child relationship and build a foundation of trust and respect. It is important for parents to prioritize their relationship with their child, and to invest time and energy into nurturing it. By focusing on communication, quality time, consistency, love and affection, and understanding and support, parents can lay the groundwork for a strong and healthy parent-child relationship that can benefit their child throughout their life. By building a strong relationship with their child, parents can help them thrive and succeed in all aspects of their development.

- Teaching children to express themselves effectively

Teaching children to express themselves effectively is a crucial aspect of their overall development. Effective communication skills are vital for success in all areas of life, from personal relationships to academic and professional endeavors. By helping children learn how to express themselves clearly and confidently, we are equipping them with a valuable tool that will serve them well throughout their lives.

One of the key elements of teaching children to express themselves effectively is creating a supportive and encouraging environment in which they feel comfortable expressing their thoughts and feelings. This can be achieved by fostering a sense of trust and open communication between the child and the adult or teacher. Encouraging children to share their thoughts and emotions without fear of judgment or criticism helps them build confidence in their ability to communicate effectively.

Another important aspect of teaching children to express themselves effectively is helping them develop active listening skills. By teaching children how to actively listen to others, we are not only helping them understand the importance of communication as a two-way process, but also enabling them to better understand and respond to the needs and feelings of others. Active listening involves paying attention to what the other person is saying, asking clarifying questions, and providing appropriate feedback.

In addition to active listening, teaching children to express themselves effectively also involves helping them build their vocabulary and communication skills. This can be achieved through a variety of activities, such as reading, writing, storytelling, and role-playing. By exposing children to a wide range of language and communication experiences, we are helping them expand their cognitive and linguistic abilities, as well as their creativity and imagination.

Furthermore, it is important to teach children the importance of nonverbal communication in expressing themselves effectively. Nonverbal cues, such as body language, facial expressions, and tone of voice, play a significant role in how our messages are perceived by others. By helping children become aware of and control their nonverbal cues, we are enabling them to communicate more effectively and authentically.

Another valuable skill in teaching children to express themselves effectively is helping them develop emotional intelligence. Emotional intelligence involves being able to recognize, understand, and manage one's own emotions, as well as being able to empathize with the emotions of others. By teaching children about emotional intelligence, we are helping them develop the skills they need to express themselves in a respectful and empathetic manner. By creating a supportive and encouraging environment, helping children develop active listening skills, building their vocabulary and language skills, teaching them about nonverbal communication, and fostering emotional intelligence, we are equipping children with the tools they need to communicate confidently and successfully in all areas of their lives. Ultimately, effective communication is a key element of a successful and fulfilling life, and by teaching children how to express themselves effectively, we are setting them up for success in the future.

Chapter 8: Encouraging Independence

- The benefits of fostering independence in children

Fostering independence in children is an essential aspect of their development that can lead to numerous benefits in their lives. Independence allows children to build self-confidence, self-reliance, and a sense of responsibility for their actions. By giving children the opportunity to make decisions and take on tasks on their own, parents and caregivers can help them develop the skills necessary to navigate the challenges of life with confidence and resilience. Research has shown that children who are encouraged to be independent from a young age are more likely to succeed academically, socially, and emotionally as they grow older.

One of the key benefits of fostering independence in children is the development of self-esteem. When children are given the chance to try new things and make decisions on their own, they gain a sense of accomplishment and pride in their abilities. This boosts their self-esteem and helps build a positive self-image. Children who are confident in their own abilities are more likely to take risks, try new things, and overcome challenges. This sense of self-worth can carry over into other areas of their lives, helping them to build strong relationships, pursue their goals, and handle setbacks with resilience.

Independence also plays a crucial role in helping children develop problem-solving skills. When children are given the space to figure things out on their own, they learn how to think critically, analyze situations, and come up with creative solutions. This ability to problem solve is a valuable skill that will serve children well throughout their lives, helping them to navigate the complexities of the world with confidence and resourcefulness. By fostering independence, parents and caregivers can empower children to take ownership of their own problems and find effective ways to address them.

Another important benefit of fostering independence in children is the development of resilience. When children are encouraged to take on tasks and responsibilities independently, they learn how to cope with challenges and setbacks in a healthy and constructive way. They develop a sense of perseverance and determination that helps them to bounce back from failures and setbacks. This resilience is a critical skill that will help children to navigate the ups and downs of life with grace and strength. By fostering independence, parents and caregivers can help children build the resilience they need to face adversity head-on and emerge stronger and more resilient.

In addition to the psychological benefits, fostering independence in children can also lead to practical advantages. Children who are independent are better equipped to take care of themselves and their belongings, manage their time effectively, and handle tasks and responsibilities on their own. This can help reduce the burden on parents and caregivers and empower children to take on more responsibilities as they grow older. Children who are independent are also more likely to succeed academically, as they are able to manage their time effectively, take initiative in their learning, and seek out resources and support when needed. By fostering independence in children, parents and caregivers can help set them up for success in school and beyond. Independence helps children build self-esteem, develop problem-solving skills, and cultivate resilience. It also leads to practical advantages, such as the ability to take care of themselves, manage their time effectively, and succeed academically. By giving children the space to make decisions and take on tasks on their own, parents and caregivers can help them develop the skills and confidence they need to thrive in an ever-changing world. Investing in independence today is an investment in the future success and well-being of children everywhere.

- Giving children age-appropriate responsibilities

Giving children age-appropriate responsibilities is a key aspect of their development and growth. It is important for parents and caregivers to understand the importance of assigning tasks and chores to children that are suitable for their age and level of maturity. By giving children responsibilities, they learn valuable life skills such as time management, organization, and accountability. These skills will benefit them in their academic and personal lives, as well as prepare them for adulthood.

When determining what responsibilities are appropriate for children, it is essential to consider their age, developmental stage, and ability. For younger children, simple tasks such as putting away toys, setting the table, or watering plants can help them develop a sense of responsibility and independence. As children get older, they can take on more complex tasks such as doing laundry, preparing meals, or caring for pets. By gradually increasing the level of responsibility given to children, parents can help them build confidence and a sense of accomplishment.

It is also important for parents to provide guidance and support when assigning responsibilities to children. Parents should clearly communicate expectations and provide instructions on how tasks should be completed. Offering praise and recognition for a job well done can motivate children to continue to take on responsibilities and strive for excellence. Additionally, parents should be patient and understanding, as children may need time to learn how to effectively complete tasks and chores.

By giving children age-appropriate responsibilities, parents can instill important values and skills that will benefit them throughout their lives. Responsibility teaches children the importance of hard work, commitment, and dedication. It also helps them develop a sense of initiative and independence, which will serve them well in school, work, and other areas of their lives. Furthermore, children who are given responsibilities are more likely to develop a positive self-esteem and a sense of purpose.

Research has shown that children who are given responsibilities from a young age are more likely to become independent and self-sufficient adults. They are better equipped to handle challenges and obstacles, and are more likely to pursue their goals with diligence and determination. By encouraging children to take on responsibilities and teaching them the necessary skills to succeed, parents are setting them up for a successful and fulfilling future. It helps them learn important life skills, instills valuable values, and prepares them for adulthood. By providing guidance and support, parents can help their children build confidence, independence, and a sense of responsibility. Ultimately, children who are given responsibilities are more likely to become successful and self-sufficient adults. Parents should strive to offer their children meaningful tasks and chores that challenge them, while also providing the necessary support and encouragement to help them succeed.

- Supporting children in making their own decisions

Supporting children in making their own decisions is a crucial aspect of their development and growth. As adults, it is natural for us to want to guide and protect children, but it is equally important to empower them to make choices and decisions for themselves. By allowing children to make their own decisions, we are helping them to develop important skills such as critical thinking, problem-solving, and self-confidence. However, it can be challenging for adults to strike the right balance between providing guidance and allowing children to take the lead. In this essay, we will explore some strategies for supporting children in making their own decisions in a way that is both respectful and nurturing.

One important aspect of supporting children in making their own decisions is to provide them with opportunities to practice decision-making skills. This could involve giving children choices in their daily activities, such as what to wear or what to eat for breakfast. By allowing children to make these small decisions, we are helping them to develop their decision-making abilities in a low-stakes environment. It is also important to encourage children to reflect on the consequences of their choices, both positive and negative. This can help them to understand the impact of their decisions and learn to make more informed choices in the future.

Another key aspect of supporting children in making their own decisions is to create a supportive and nurturing environment. This involves providing children with the guidance and resources they need to make decisions, while also respecting their autonomy and individuality. Adults can offer advice and guidance to children, but ultimately it is important to allow them to make their own choices and learn from their experiences. It is also essential to create a safe space for children to express their thoughts and feelings, without fear of judgment or criticism. This can help children to feel empowered and confident in making their own decisions.

It is also important to recognize that children may need support and guidance from adults in making decisions that are more complex or challenging. In these situations, adults can help children to break down the decision-making process into smaller steps, and provide them with the information and resources they need to make an informed choice. Adults can also help children to consider the perspectives of others and think about how their decisions may impact those around them. By involving children in the decision-making process and empowering them to take the lead, adults can help children to develop important life skills that will serve them well in the future. By providing children with opportunities to practice decision-making skills, creating a supportive and nurturing environment, and recognizing when children may need guidance and support, adults can help children to develop important skills such as critical thinking, problem-solving, and self-confidence. Ultimately, by empowering children to make their own decisions, we are helping them to become independent and responsible individuals who are capable of navigating the complexities of the world around them.

Chapter 9: Nurturing Emotional Intelligence

- The role of emotional intelligence in confidence-building

Confidence-building is a critical aspect of personal and professional success, as it enables individuals to take risks, overcome challenges, and achieve their goals. One key factor that significantly contributes to confidence-building is emotional intelligence. Emotional intelligence, often referred to as EQ, is the ability to recognize, understand, and manage our own emotions, as well as the emotions of others. This skill set plays a crucial role in how we perceive and react to situations, make decisions, build relationships, and navigate various social and professional environments.

Emotional intelligence is comprised of several core components, including self-awareness, self-regulation, social awareness, and relationship management. Self-awareness involves the ability to recognize and understand our own emotions, thoughts, and values. This awareness enables us to accurately assess our strengths and weaknesses, as well as how our emotions influence our behavior and decision-making processes. Self-regulation, on the other hand, involves managing our emotions and impulses in a constructive and adaptive manner. By effectively regulating our emotions, we can control our reactions, make rational decisions, and maintain a sense of composure in challenging situations.

Social awareness refers to the ability to empathize and understand the emotions and perspectives of others. This skill set allows us to accurately perceive social cues, read nonverbal communication, and navigate interpersonal dynamics effectively. Socially aware individuals are able to build and maintain positive relationships, collaborate with others, and demonstrate empathy and understanding towards others. Lastly, relationship management involves using emotional intelligence to establish and maintain healthy and productive relationships with others. This component encompasses skills such as effective communication, conflict resolution, teamwork, and the ability to inspire and influence others.

When it comes to confidence-building, emotional intelligence plays a significant role in enhancing our self-perception and belief in our abilities. By developing a high level of self-awareness, individuals can recognize their strengths and weaknesses, understand their emotions, and accurately assess their skills and competencies. This self-awareness enables them to set realistic goals, make informed decisions, and take appropriate actions to achieve success. Additionally, by mastering self-regulation, individuals can effectively manage their fears, doubts, and insecurities, and maintain a positive and optimistic mindset in the face of challenges and setbacks.

Furthermore, emotional intelligence helps individuals develop strong social connections and establish positive relationships with others. By cultivating social awareness, individuals can empathize with others, build rapport, and foster trust and mutual respect. These positive social connections provide a strong support system, enhance motivation and morale, and boost confidence in one's abilities. Relationship management skills, such as effective communication and conflict resolution, also play a vital role in building confidence by enabling individuals to assert themselves, express their needs and opinions, and navigate interpersonal dynamics successfully. By developing these key components of emotional intelligence, individuals can gain a deeper understanding of themselves, effectively manage their emotions, empathize with others, and establish positive relationships. These skills enable individuals to build and maintain their self-confidence, navigate challenges and setbacks, and achieve their goals with resilience and determination. Ultimately, emotional intelligence serves as a powerful tool for enhancing confidence, empowering individuals to thrive in both personal and professional aspects of their lives.

- Helping children identify and regulate emotions

Emotions play a critical role in children's development and well-being. Learning to identify and regulate emotions is a crucial skill that can have long-lasting effects on a child's social and emotional development. Children who are able to recognize and manage their emotions are better equipped to navigate the challenges of everyday life, maintain positive relationships, and cope with stress and adversity. As educators, parents, and caregivers, it is our responsibility to support children in developing these essential skills.

One of the first steps in helping children identify and regulate their emotions is to create a safe and supportive environment where they feel comfortable expressing their feelings. Children need to know that it is okay to feel a wide range of emotions, and that their feelings are valid. Encouraging open communication and empathy can help children develop a healthy emotional awareness and vocabulary. By actively listening to children's feelings and experiences, we can validate their emotions and help them understand and articulate what they are feeling.

It is also important to teach children about different emotions and how to recognize them in themselves and others. By using age-appropriate language and examples, we can help children learn to identify and label their emotions, such as happiness, sadness, anger, fear, and excitement. Teaching children to recognize the physical signs of different emotions, such as changes in facial expressions, body language, and tone of voice, can also help them become more aware of their own emotional state.

Once children have a basic understanding of emotions, it is important to help them learn how to regulate their feelings in healthy and constructive ways. This involves teaching children coping strategies and self-regulation techniques that they can use to manage their emotions and behavior. For example, deep breathing exercises, mindfulness techniques, and positive self-talk can help children calm themselves down when they are feeling overwhelmed or upset. Encouraging children to engage in activities that promote relaxation and self-care, such as exercising, drawing, or listening to music, can also help them regulate their emotions and reduce stress.

It is important for adults to model positive emotional regulation skills for children by managing their own emotions effectively. Children learn by example, so it is essential for parents, educators, and caregivers to demonstrate healthy coping strategies and communication styles in their own interactions with children. By showing children how to express and regulate emotions in a constructive and respectful manner, we can help them develop the skills they need to navigate their own emotions in a positive way. By creating a supportive environment, teaching children about different emotions, and providing them with the tools and strategies they need to manage their feelings, we can empower children to become emotionally resilient and empathetic individuals. By fostering emotional awareness and self-regulation in children, we can help them build strong relationships, navigate challenges, and thrive in all aspects of their lives.

- Encouraging empathy and compassion

Empathy and compassion are vital components of the human experience, essential for fostering connections with others and building a more compassionate society. Encouraging empathy and compassion in ourselves and others is crucial for promoting understanding, acceptance, and kindness towards those around us. In this essay, we will explore the importance of empathy and compassion, the factors that influence our ability to empathize and show compassion, and strategies for cultivating empathy and compassion in our daily lives.

Empathy is the ability to understand and share the feelings of others. It involves putting ourselves in someone else's shoes and seeing the world from their perspective. Compassion, on the other hand, is the desire to alleviate the suffering of others and the willingness to take action to help them. Empathy and compassion go hand in hand, as empathy allows us to connect with others on an emotional level, while compassion motivates us to take steps to alleviate their pain or suffering.

There are several factors that can influence our ability to empathize and show compassion. These include our upbringing, personality traits, past experiences, cultural background, and social influences. For example, individuals who were raised in a supportive and loving environment are more likely to develop strong empathy and compassion skills, as they have been shown kindness and understanding from a young age. Similarly, people who have experienced hardship or adversity in their lives may be more empathetic and compassionate towards others going through similar challenges.

In addition to our personal experiences, our cultural background also plays a significant role in shaping our capacity for empathy and compassion. Different cultures may have varying norms and values surrounding empathy and compassion, which can impact how individuals express these emotions. For example, some cultures may prioritize individualism and self-reliance, while others may emphasize collectivism and community support. Understanding and respecting these cultural differences is crucial for promoting empathy and compassion on a global scale.

Despite the various factors that can influence our ability to empathize and show compassion, it is important to recognize that empathy and compassion are skills that can be developed and strengthened over time. By actively practicing empathy and compassion in our daily lives, we can cultivate a greater sense of connection and understanding with those around us. This can help us build stronger relationships, promote positive social change, and create a more compassionate and inclusive society.

There are several strategies that we can use to cultivate empathy and compassion in ourselves and others. One important approach is to actively listen and validate the feelings of others. By taking the time to listen to someone's concerns and emotions without judgement, we can show that we care about their well-being and are willing to support them in their time of need. This can help foster a sense of trust and openness in our relationships, leading to greater empathy and compassion.

Another strategy for promoting empathy and compassion is to practice gratitude and kindness towards others. By expressing gratitude for the positive things in our lives and showing kindness to those around us, we can create a more positive and empathetic outlook on life. Small acts of kindness, such as offering a helping hand to a friend in need or volunteering in our community, can go a long way in promoting empathy and compassion towards others.

In addition, it is important to challenge our own biases and stereotypes in order to cultivate empathy and compassion. By recognizing and confronting our own prejudices and preconceived notions about others, we can open ourselves up to understanding and empathizing with people of different backgrounds and experiences. This can help us break down barriers and promote greater inclusivity and acceptance in our communities. By actively practicing empathy and compassion in our daily lives, we can foster understanding, acceptance, and kindness towards those around us. By listening, validating, and supporting others, practicing gratitude and kindness, and challenging our own biases, we can cultivate empathy and compassion within ourselves and inspire others to do the same. Together, we can create a more empathetic and compassionate world for all.

Chapter 10: Creating a Supportive Environment

- The impact of the home environment on children's self-esteem

Self-esteem is a critical aspect of a child's development, shaping their thoughts, feelings, and behaviors. The home environment plays a significant role in influencing children's self-esteem, as it is their primary social context during their formative years. The interactions, relationships, and experiences they have within their home can either nurture or hinder the development of a healthy self-esteem. This paper will explore the impact of the home environment on children's self-esteem, focusing on the various factors that can either support or undermine this crucial aspect of their psychological well-being.

One of the key factors that can influence a child's self-esteem is the quality of the parent-child relationship. Children who have secure attachments with their caregivers tend to develop higher levels of self-esteem, as they feel valued, supported, and loved. Positive interactions with parents, such as praise, encouragement, and affection, can help children build a strong sense of self-worth and confidence. On the other hand, children who experience neglect, rejection, or abuse from their parents may develop low self-esteem, as they internalize negative beliefs about themselves. The way parents communicate with their children, set boundaries, and provide emotional support can all impact their self-esteem in profound ways.

In addition to the parent-child relationship, the overall emotional climate of the home can also shape a child's self-esteem. A home environment that is characterized by warmth, stability, and emotional security is more likely to foster healthy self-esteem in children. When children feel safe, valued, and respected in their home, they are more likely to develop a positive self-concept and a sense of belonging. Conversely, a home environment that is marked by conflict, instability, or dysfunction can have a detrimental impact on children's self-esteem. Exposure to domestic violence, substance abuse, or other forms of adversity can erode children's self-esteem and lead to feelings of worthlessness or inadequacy.

The role of siblings and other family members should also be considered when examining the impact of the home environment on children's self-esteem. Siblings can either be sources of support and encouragement or sources of conflict and rivalry, depending on the nature of their relationship. Positive sibling relationships can contribute to a child's sense of social connectedness and self-worth, while negative interactions can undermine their self-esteem. Similarly, the presence of extended family members, such as grandparents, aunts, uncles, and cousins, can provide additional sources of emotional support and validation for children, which can bolster their self-esteem. Family dynamics and the quality of relationships among family members can have a profound influence on children's self-esteem.

The physical environment of the home can also impact children's self-esteem. A safe, clean, and organized living space can promote feelings of security and well-being in children, whereas a chaotic or cluttered environment may contribute to feelings of stress and anxiety. The design and layout of the home, as well as the availability of resources and amenities, can also influence children's self-esteem. Children who live in comfortable, aesthetically pleasing homes may feel a greater sense of pride and satisfaction, while those who lack basic necessities or live in overcrowded or substandard conditions may experience feelings of shame or inadequacy. The physical environment of the home can shape children's perceptions of themselves and their place in the world.

Furthermore, the cultural and socio-economic context of the home can impact children's self-esteem in significant ways. Children who grow up in families that value education, achievement, and personal growth are more likely to develop a strong sense of self-esteem, as they receive positive messages about their abilities and potential. On the other hand, children who are raised in environments where negative stereotypes, prejudice, or discrimination are prevalent may internalize harmful beliefs about themselves and their worth. Socio-economic factors, such as poverty, unemployment, or lack of access to resources, can also impact children's self-esteem, as they may be more likely to experience feelings of powerlessness, shame, or inferiority. The cultural and socio-economic context of the home can shape children's self-esteem in complex ways, influencing their beliefs about themselves and their place in society. The quality of the parent-child relationship, the emotional climate of the home, the role of siblings and family members, the physical environment of the home, and the cultural and socio-economic context all contribute to children's self-esteem. By creating a supportive, nurturing, and empowering home environment, parents and caregivers can help children develop a strong sense of self-worth, confidence, and resilience. Understanding the impact of the home environment on children's self-esteem is essential for promoting positive psychological development and well-being in young people.

- Strategies for promoting a supportive and nurturing environment

Creating a supportive and nurturing environment in any setting, whether it be a workplace, classroom, or community, is essential for fostering growth, well-being, and productivity among individuals. As such, it is crucial for leaders and individuals in positions of authority to employ various strategies to promote such an environment. By doing so, they can help cultivate a positive culture that encourages collaboration, creativity, and overall success.

One of the key strategies for promoting a supportive and nurturing environment is effective communication. Clear and open communication is the foundation of any healthy relationship or environment. Leaders must ensure that they maintain transparency with their team members, providing them with clear expectations, feedback, and guidance. By fostering open lines of communication, individuals feel empowered to express their ideas, concerns, and emotions, creating a sense of trust and respect within the group.

Another important strategy for promoting a supportive environment is to prioritize the well-being of individuals. This involves acknowledging the personal needs and challenges of team members and providing them with the necessary support to navigate through them. Leaders should take the time to check in on the mental and emotional well-being of their team members, offering resources such as counseling or mindfulness practices to promote a healthy work-life balance. By prioritizing well-being, individuals feel valued, supported, and motivated to perform at their best.

In addition to effective communication and prioritizing well-being, leaders can promote a supportive environment by fostering a sense of community and belonging among team members. This can be achieved through team-building activities, social gatherings, or volunteer opportunities that bring individuals together outside of their usual work tasks. By creating opportunities for individuals to connect and build relationships with one another, leaders can cultivate a sense of camaraderie that promotes collaboration, cooperation, and empathy within the group.

Furthermore, promoting a supportive environment involves recognizing and celebrating the achievements and successes of individuals. By acknowledging and rewarding the hard work and dedication of team members, leaders can boost morale, motivation, and confidence among individuals. This can be done through public recognition, awards, or incentives that demonstrate appreciation for the contributions of team members. By celebrating successes, individuals feel valued, acknowledged, and inspired to continue striving for excellence. By fostering a positive culture that promotes collaboration, creativity, and overall success, leaders can cultivate an environment where individuals feel empowered, valued, and motivated to reach their full potential. Through these strategies, leaders can create a culture of support and encouragement that fosters growth, development, and well-being among individuals in any setting.

- Building a network of positive influences

Building a network of positive influences is essential for personal and professional growth. Surrounding yourself with individuals who inspire, support, and motivate you can have a profound impact on your success and well-being. Positive influences can come from a variety of sources, such as friends, family members, colleagues, mentors, and even online communities. These individuals can offer guidance, encouragement, and constructive feedback, helping you navigate challenges and achieve your goals.

One of the key benefits of building a network of positive influences is the opportunity for learning and growth. When you surround yourself with people who have diverse backgrounds, experiences, and perspectives, you are exposed to new ideas and ways of thinking. This can broaden your own understanding of the world and challenge you to step outside of your comfort zone. Positive influences can also serve as role models, showing you what is possible and inspiring you to reach new heights in your personal and professional life.

In addition to offering support and guidance, a network of positive influences can provide valuable opportunities for collaboration and networking. By connecting with like-minded individuals who share your values and goals, you can form partnerships and alliances that can help you advance your career or pursue new opportunities. Positive influences can introduce you to new contacts, mentor you in your field, or provide referrals that can open doors to exciting possibilities. Building a strong network of positive influences can increase your visibility and credibility in your professional community, enhancing your chances of success.

Another important aspect of building a network of positive influences is the impact it can have on your mental and emotional well-being. Surrounding yourself with individuals who uplift and encourage you can boost your confidence, self-esteem, and resilience. Positive influences can serve as a source of emotional support when you are facing challenges or setbacks, helping you stay motivated and focused on your goals. By cultivating relationships with people who believe in you and your potential, you can create a supportive environment that nurtures your personal growth and development.

To build a network of positive influences, it is important to be proactive and intentional in seeking out individuals who align with your values and aspirations. Start by identifying the qualities and traits you admire in others, such as kindness, empathy, creativity, or professionalism. Look for opportunities to connect with people who possess these qualities, whether it is through networking events, professional organizations, social media platforms, or community groups. Be open to new relationships and be willing to invest time and effort in nurturing them. Building a network of positive influences is a gradual process that requires patience, persistence, and genuine interest in others.

Once you have established connections with individuals who uplift and inspire you, make an effort to cultivate these relationships through regular communication, collaboration, and mutual support. Show appreciation for their contributions to your life and career, and offer your own support and encouragement in return. Be a good listener, show empathy and understanding, and be willing to offer help and assistance when needed. By building strong and meaningful relationships with positive influences, you can create a supportive and nurturing environment that fosters your growth and success. Surrounding yourself with individuals who inspire, support, and uplift you can have a transformative impact on your life, helping you navigate challenges, achieve your goals, and maintain a positive outlook. By seeking out like-minded individuals who share your values and aspirations, and nurturing these relationships with care and intention, you can create a supportive network that empowers you to reach your full potential. Remember that building a network of positive influences is a continuous process that requires effort, but the rewards of having a strong and supportive community by your side are immeasurable.

Chapter 11: Mindfulness and Self-Care

- Introducing children to mindfulness practices

Introducing children to mindfulness practices is a topic of growing interest and importance in the field of child development and education. Mindfulness, which can be described as the practice of being present in the moment and aware of one's thoughts and feelings without judgment, has been shown to have numerous benefits for both children and adults.

One of the key ways to introduce children to mindfulness practices is through simple exercises that help them develop their awareness of their thoughts and emotions. These exercises can be as simple as asking children to take a few deep breaths and notice how their body feels, or guiding them through a body scan to help them become more aware of their physical sensations. By regularly practicing these exercises, children can learn to pause and reflect on their internal experiences, rather than reacting impulsively to their emotions.

Another important aspect of introducing children to mindfulness practices is creating a supportive and nurturing environment where they feel comfortable exploring their thoughts and emotions. This can be achieved by incorporating mindfulness activities into daily routines, such as during circle time at school or before bedtime at home. By normalizing mindfulness practices and emphasizing their importance, children can begin to see them as a natural part of their daily life.

In addition to incorporating mindfulness into daily routines, it is also important to teach children about the benefits of mindfulness and how it can help them in their daily lives. This can be done through storytelling, role-playing, or engaging in mindfulness exercises together as a group.

It is also important to consider the developmental stage of the child when introducing mindfulness practices. Young children may benefit from simple activities such as coloring mandalas or practicing mindful breathing, while older children may be more interested in exploring mindfulness through journaling or guided meditations. By tailoring mindfulness practices to the child's age and interests, educators and parents can ensure that the practices are engaging and relevant to the child's needs.

Furthermore, it is important to model mindfulness practices for children by practicing them consistently and authentically. Children learn by example, so by demonstrating mindfulness in our own lives, we can show children how to incorporate it into their own daily routines. This can be achieved by engaging in mindfulness practices together as a family or with a group of peers, creating a sense of shared experience and connection. By incorporating mindfulness activities into daily routines, creating a supportive environment for exploration, and teaching children about the benefits of mindfulness, we can help children cultivate a sense of self-awareness, emotional regulation, and resilience that will serve them well throughout their lives.

- Teaching self-care habits and routines

Self-care is a crucial component of maintaining overall well-being and mental health. Teaching self-care habits and routines to individuals is essential in helping them develop positive coping mechanisms and strategies to navigate the challenges of everyday life. Self-care encompasses a range of practices that promote physical, emotional, and mental health, such as healthy eating, exercise, mindfulness, and stress management. By imparting these skills to others, educators can empower individuals to take control of their own health and well-being.

One of the first steps in teaching self-care habits and routines is to educate individuals about the importance of self-care and its impact on overall health. Many people may not fully understand the connection between self-care and well-being, and may not prioritize self-care in their daily lives. By providing information on the benefits of self-care, such as reduced stress, improved emotional well-being, and increased energy levels, educators can help individuals recognize the value of incorporating self-care practices into their daily routines.

In addition to educating individuals about the benefits of self-care, it is important to teach practical self-care strategies that individuals can easily implement into their daily routines. This may include techniques such as setting aside time for exercise, practicing mindfulness and meditation, maintaining a healthy diet, getting enough sleep, and engaging in activities that bring joy and relaxation. By teaching individuals how to incorporate these practices into their daily lives, educators can help them develop a strong foundation for self-care that will benefit them in the long term.

Furthermore, it is important to emphasize the importance of self-care as a proactive rather than reactive practice. Self-care should be viewed as a holistic approach to maintaining health and well-being, rather than as a response to stress or crisis. By teaching individuals to prioritize self-care as a daily practice, educators can help them build resilience and coping skills that will enable them to better navigate life's challenges and stressors.

It is also important to address common barriers to self-care that individuals may face, such as time constraints, financial limitations, and lack of knowledge or motivation. Educators can help individuals overcome these barriers by providing practical tips and resources for incorporating self-care into their daily routines, regardless of their circumstances. This may include simple strategies such as scheduling self-care activities in advance, setting realistic goals, and seeking support from friends, family, or professional resources. By educating individuals about the benefits of self-care, teaching practical strategies for incorporating self-care practices into daily routines, emphasizing the proactive nature of self-care, and addressing common barriers to self-care, educators can empower individuals to take control of their own health and well-being. By instilling a strong foundation of self-care skills and practices, educators can help individuals build resilience, cope effectively with stress, and lead healthier and happier lives.

- The importance of self-care for overall well-being

Self-care is a crucial aspect of maintaining overall well-being, encompassing physical, emotional, and mental health. It involves taking deliberate actions to care for oneself and prioritize personal needs. Self-care is not a selfish act; rather, it is a necessary practice that allows individuals to sustain their energy, improve their mood, and enhance their relationships. It is a fundamental component of a healthy lifestyle and plays a significant role in preventing burnout and stress-related illnesses.

One of the key benefits of self-care is its ability to improve overall physical health. Making time for exercise, getting an adequate amount of sleep, and eating a balanced diet are all essential components of self-care. These practices not only contribute to physical health but also have a positive impact on mental well-being. Engaging in activities that promote physical health, such as yoga, running, or swimming, can help alleviate stress and anxiety, improve mood, and boost self-esteem. Prioritizing physical self-care can also prevent chronic illnesses and improve overall quality of life.

In addition to physical health, self-care is crucial for maintaining emotional well-being. Engaging in activities that bring joy, such as spending time with loved ones, pursuing hobbies, or practicing mindfulness, can help individuals manage stress and cultivate a positive mindset. Taking time to relax and unwind is essential for emotional health, as it allows individuals to recharge and rejuvenate. Emotional self-care also involves setting boundaries, expressing emotions, and seeking support when needed. By prioritizing emotional well-being, individuals can develop resilience, cope with challenges, and cultivate a sense of inner peace.

Furthermore, self-care plays a vital role in maintaining mental health. Engaging in activities that stimulate the mind, such as reading, learning new skills, or practicing mindfulness, can improve cognitive function and enhance mental clarity. Taking time for self-reflection and introspection is also important for mental well-being, as it allows individuals to identify their needs, values, and goals. Mental self-care involves managing stress, practicing self-compassion, and seeking professional help when needed. By prioritizing mental health, individuals can improve their focus, creativity, and decision-making skills.

Self-care is not a luxury but a necessity for overall well-being. It is a proactive approach to managing stress, preventing burnout, and enhancing quality of life. By prioritizing self-care, individuals can improve their physical, emotional, and mental health, leading to greater resilience, happiness, and fulfillment. It is essential for individuals to make self-care a regular practice in their daily lives, as it is an investment in their well-being and happiness. By taking care of oneself, individuals can better care for others and contribute positively to their communities and the world at large.

Chapter 12: Social Skills and Relationships

- Importance of social skills in building confidence

Social skills play a crucial role in building confidence and establishing positive relationships with others. Confidence is an essential aspect of a person's overall well-being and success in both personal and professional settings. It allows individuals to believe in themselves, their abilities, and their worth, enabling them to face challenges with courage and resilience. Social skills, on the other hand, refer to the ability to communicate effectively, interact with others, and navigate social situations with ease. When combined, confidence and social skills create a powerful combination that can lead to increased self-esteem, improved relationships, and greater success in various aspects of life.

One of the key reasons why social skills are important in building confidence is that they enable individuals to form meaningful connections with others. Being able to communicate effectively, actively listen, and show empathy towards others are all essential components of successful interpersonal relationships. By mastering these social skills, individuals can establish rapport with others, foster trust, and create a sense of connection that can boost their self-esteem and confidence. In social interactions, confidence is often perceived by others as a sign of competence and reliability, which can further strengthen relationships and validate one's sense of self-worth.

Additionally, social skills play a significant role in helping individuals navigate social situations and handle conflict effectively. In interpersonal interactions, misunderstandings and disagreements are bound to occur, and having strong social skills can help individuals approach these situations with confidence and maturity. By being able to communicate clearly, assert their needs, and resolve conflicts in a constructive manner, individuals can build their self-confidence and maintain positive relationships with others. Moreover, social skills can also help individuals navigate group dynamics, such as leadership roles, teamwork, and collaboration, which are essential in many professional settings.

Furthermore, social skills can also help individuals overcome social anxiety and shyness, which can often hinder their confidence levels. By developing effective communication skills, assertiveness, and emotional intelligence, individuals can feel more comfortable and confident in social situations. For example, learning how to engage in small talk, express oneself clearly, and establish boundaries can all contribute to building confidence and reducing feelings of awkwardness or self-doubt. Additionally, social skills training can provide individuals with the tools and techniques to manage anxiety-provoking situations, such as public speaking, networking events, or social gatherings, which can further boost their confidence and self-assurance.

In the realm of professional settings, social skills are essential for building confidence and advancing one's career. Strong communication skills, leadership abilities, and networking capabilities are highly sought after traits in the workplace, and employees who possess these skills are more likely to succeed and excel in their roles. By honing their social skills, individuals can improve their ability to collaborate with others, negotiate effectively, and build strong relationships with colleagues, clients, and stakeholders. This can lead to increased job satisfaction, opportunities for career advancement, and recognition for their contributions, all of which can bolster their confidence and sense of professional fulfillment. By mastering the art of effective communication, interpersonal skills, and emotional intelligence, individuals can increase their self-esteem, navigate social situations with ease, and create meaningful connections with others. In personal and professional settings, confidence is a key factor in achieving success, and social skills are the foundation upon which this confidence is built. By developing and refining these skills, individuals can unlock their full potential, build strong relationships, and succeed in all aspects of their lives.

- Teaching children how to make and maintain friendships

Friendships play a crucial role in a child's social and emotional development. Learning how to make and maintain friendships is a skill that can greatly impact a child's overall well-being and happiness. As a teacher or parent, it is important to guide children in developing these skills from a young age. By providing children with the necessary tools and knowledge, they can build meaningful connections with their peers and foster positive relationships that can last a lifetime.

One of the first steps in teaching children how to make and maintain friendships is helping them understand the importance of empathy and kindness. Empathy is the ability to understand and share the feelings of others, while kindness involves showing compassion and consideration towards others. By teaching children to be empathetic and kind, they can form deeper connections with their peers and cultivate a sense of mutual respect and understanding. Encouraging children to put themselves in others' shoes and consider how their actions may impact others is a valuable lesson that can help them navigate social interactions with sensitivity and thoughtfulness.

Another important aspect of teaching children how to make and maintain friendships is helping them develop effective communication skills. Communication is essential in building and sustaining relationships, as it allows individuals to express their thoughts, feelings, and needs. Teaching children how to communicate effectively, both verbally and non-verbally, can help them navigate social situations with confidence and clarity. Encouraging children to listen actively, ask questions, and express themselves honestly can empower them to communicate effectively with their peers and establish strong and meaningful connections.

In addition to empathy and communication, teaching children how to make and maintain friendships also involves helping them develop conflict resolution skills. Conflicts are a natural part of any relationship, and learning how to navigate disagreements and misunderstandings in a constructive manner is essential for maintaining healthy friendships. Teaching children strategies for resolving conflicts peacefully, such as active listening, compromise, and perspective-taking, can help them address disagreements and build stronger relationships with their peers. By equipping children with the skills to manage conflicts effectively, they can learn to communicate openly, address issues head-on, and work towards finding mutually beneficial solutions.

Furthermore, it is important to teach children the importance of boundaries and respect in friendships. Boundaries help individuals establish and maintain healthy relationships by setting clear expectations for behavior and interactions. Teaching children to respect others' boundaries and communicate their own boundaries can help them navigate friendships with respect and consideration. By fostering a culture of mutual respect and understanding, children can create safe and supportive environments where they can express themselves authentically and build trusting relationships with their peers. By equipping children with empathy, communication, conflict resolution, and boundary-setting skills, they can develop meaningful connections with their peers and nurture positive and supportive relationships. As educators and parents, it is important to guide and support children in honing these skills from a young age, so they can navigate social interactions with confidence, respect, and kindness. Ultimately, teaching children how to make and maintain friendships is an essential aspect of their social and emotional development, and it can help them cultivate positive and fulfilling relationships that can enrich their lives for years to come.

- Respecting boundaries and handling conflicts

Respecting boundaries and handling conflicts are essential skills in maintaining healthy relationships, whether they be personal or professional. Boundaries are the limits we set for ourselves and others in terms of what is acceptable behavior or not. When these boundaries are crossed, conflicts can arise. It is important to understand and respect the boundaries of others while also asserting our own boundaries in a clear and assertive manner.

One key aspect of respecting boundaries is communication. Effective communication is essential in setting and maintaining boundaries. This involves clearly expressing what is and is not acceptable to us, as well as listening to and respecting the boundaries of others. It is important to remember that boundaries are not set in stone and can evolve over time. Therefore, ongoing communication is crucial to ensure that boundaries are respected and conflicts are minimized.

In handling conflicts that may arise when boundaries are crossed, it is important to approach the situation with a calm and rational mindset. Emotions can often cloud judgment and escalate conflicts, so it is important to take a step back and assess the situation objectively. It is also important to be open to feedback and willing to compromise in order to find a resolution that is acceptable to all parties involved.

Conflict resolution techniques such as active listening, empathy, and problem-solving skills can be helpful in handling conflicts in a constructive manner. Active listening involves fully concentrating on what the other person is saying without interrupting, while empathy involves understanding and acknowledging the feelings of others. Problem-solving skills can help in finding mutually beneficial solutions to conflicts that respect the boundaries of all parties involved.

It is also important to seek support from others when handling conflicts. This can involve enlisting the help of a mediator, counselor, or trusted friend or colleague to provide perspective and guidance in resolving the conflict. Seeking support can help in ensuring that boundaries are respected and conflicts are handled in a healthy and productive manner. Effective communication, calm and rational mindset, active listening, empathy, problem-solving skills, and seeking support are all important aspects of respecting boundaries and handling conflicts. By cultivating these skills and approaches, we can ensure that our relationships are built on mutual respect, understanding, and cooperation.

Chapter 13: Encouraging Healthy Risk-Taking

- Understanding the benefits of taking calculated risks

Taking calculated risks is a fundamental aspect of both personal and professional development. While the idea of risk-taking may evoke feelings of uncertainty and fear, it is important to understand that not all risks are created equal. Calculated risks involve a strategic approach to decision-making, where the potential benefits are carefully weighed against the possible downsides. In this way, individuals and organizations can leverage risk-taking as a tool for growth and innovation, rather than simply as a gamble.

One of the key benefits of taking calculated risks is the potential for growth and improvement. By stepping outside of one's comfort zone and pushing boundaries, individuals can challenge themselves to learn new skills, acquire new knowledge, and develop a deeper understanding of themselves and their capabilities. In a professional setting, taking calculated risks can lead to increased creativity and innovation, as individuals are encouraged to think outside the box and explore new possibilities. This can lead to new opportunities for growth, both personally and professionally, as individuals are able to expand their skill set and take on new challenges.

Another benefit of taking calculated risks is the potential for increased productivity and efficiency. When individuals are willing to take risks and try new things, they are more likely to discover better and more efficient ways of doing things. This can lead to increased productivity, as individuals are able to streamline processes and eliminate inefficiencies. In a professional setting, this can lead to improved performance and results, as individuals are able to find new ways to approach challenges and achieve their goals. By taking calculated risks, individuals can also increase their confidence and self-esteem, as they are able to see the positive results of their actions and feel a sense of accomplishment.

In addition to fostering growth and productivity, taking calculated risks can also lead to increased resilience and adaptability. When individuals are willing to take risks and step outside of their comfort zone, they become more adept at navigating uncertainty and handling setbacks. This can help individuals to develop a more positive mindset, as they are able to see failures and challenges as opportunities for growth and learning. In a professional setting, this can be particularly valuable, as individuals are able to bounce back from setbacks and adapt to changing circumstances. By taking calculated risks, individuals can also develop a more proactive and strategic approach to decision-making, as they are able to anticipate potential obstacles and plan for contingencies.

One of the most compelling benefits of taking calculated risks is the potential for greater success and achievement. By taking risks and seizing opportunities, individuals can position themselves for greater success and advancement in their personal and professional lives. In a professional setting, taking calculated risks can lead to increased recognition and opportunities for promotion, as individuals are able to demonstrate their ability to think strategically and take decisive action. This can result in greater job satisfaction and financial rewards, as individuals are able to achieve their goals and fulfill their potential. By taking calculated risks, individuals can also expand their network and build valuable relationships, as they are able to demonstrate their willingness to take on challenges and seek out new opportunities. By approaching risk-taking with a strategic mindset and weighing the potential benefits against the possible downsides, individuals and organizations can harness the power of risk-taking as a tool for growth and innovation. With the potential for increased growth, productivity, resilience, and success, the benefits of taking calculated risks are clear. By embracing uncertainty and stepping outside of one's comfort zone, individuals can position themselves for greater success and fulfillment in their personal and professional lives.

- Encouraging children to step out of their comfort zones

Encouraging children to step out of their comfort zones is crucial for their personal growth and development. Comfort zones are environments or situations in which individuals feel secure, safe, and at ease. While comfort zones can provide a sense of stability and familiarity, they can also hinder a child's ability to explore new opportunities, learn new skills, and overcome challenges. By encouraging children to step out of their comfort zones, parents, educators, and caregivers can help them develop resilience, self-confidence, and a growth mindset.

One way to encourage children to step out of their comfort zones is to provide them with opportunities to try new activities or experiences. This could involve signing them up for a new sport or hobby, enrolling them in a class that challenges them intellectually, or taking them on a trip to a new and unfamiliar place. By exposing children to different experiences, parents and caregivers can help them expand their horizons, discover new interests, and build their confidence.

Another strategy for encouraging children to step out of their comfort zones is to praise and reward their efforts and achievements. When children take risks and try new things, it is important to acknowledge their courage and perseverance. Positive reinforcement can help children feel more confident and motivated to continue stepping out of their comfort zones in the future. By celebrating their successes, parents and caregivers can show children that taking risks and facing challenges is worthwhile and rewarding.

In addition to providing opportunities and positive reinforcement, parents and caregivers can also model stepping out of their own comfort zones for children. Children learn by observing the behavior of the adults around them, so it is important for parents and caregivers to demonstrate a willingness to take risks, try new things, and face challenges themselves. By showing children that it is normal and beneficial to step out of one's comfort zone, parents and caregivers can inspire them to do the same.

It is also important to support children emotionally as they step out of their comfort zones. Encouraging words, reassurance, and empathy can help children feel more comfortable and confident as they face new challenges. It is natural for children to feel nervous, anxious, or even scared when trying something new, so it is important for parents and caregivers to provide emotional support and encouragement. By being there for children as they step out of their comfort zones, parents and caregivers can help them navigate their fears and uncertainties and build their resilience. By providing opportunities, praising their efforts, modeling stepping out of one's own comfort zone, and offering emotional support, parents and caregivers can help children expand their horizons, build their confidence, and develop a willingness to take risks and face challenges. Stepping out of one's comfort zone is not always easy, but with the right support and encouragement, children can learn to embrace new experiences, grow from their mistakes, and become more resilient and self-assured individuals.

- Building resilience through challenging experiences

Building resilience through challenging experiences is a crucial aspect of personal development and growth. Resilience can be defined as the ability to bounce back from setbacks, adapt to change, and persevere in the face of adversity. It is an essential quality to possess in today's fast-paced and unpredictable world. Challenging experiences are inevitable in life, and it is how we respond to these experiences that shapes our resilience. By navigating through difficult situations, we can not only build our resilience but also develop important life skills such as problem-solving, emotional regulation, and coping strategies.

One of the key ways in which challenging experiences can build resilience is by forcing us to confront our fears and step outside of our comfort zones. When faced with a difficult situation, we are often forced to confront our fears and push ourselves to overcome obstacles. This can be a scary and uncomfortable process, but it is through facing our fears that we grow stronger and more resilient. By stepping outside of our comfort zones and taking risks, we can develop a sense of self-efficacy and confidence in our ability to overcome challenges.

Another way in which challenging experiences can build resilience is by teaching us important coping strategies and problem-solving skills. When faced with a difficult situation, it is important to find healthy ways to cope with stress and manage our emotions. This may involve seeking support from friends and family, practicing mindfulness and relaxation techniques, or engaging in physical exercise. By developing effective coping strategies, we can build our resilience and learn how to navigate through difficult times with grace and composure.

Additionally, challenging experiences can help us develop a growth mindset, which is essential for building resilience. A growth mindset is the belief that our abilities and intelligence can be developed through hard work, effort, and perseverance. When faced with a difficult situation, individuals with a growth mindset are more likely to see it as an opportunity for growth and learning, rather than a setback or failure. By cultivating a growth mindset, we can build our resilience and approach challenges with optimism and determination.

It is important to note that building resilience through challenging experiences is not always easy or straightforward. It can be a long and difficult process, requiring patience, effort, and self-reflection. However, the benefits of developing resilience are immense and can have a positive impact on all aspects of our lives. By building resilience, we can become better equipped to deal with the inevitable ups and downs of life, navigate through difficult times with grace and resilience. By facing our fears, developing coping strategies, and cultivating a growth mindset, we can build our resilience and learn how to navigate through difficult times with grace and composure. While the process of building resilience may be challenging, the benefits are well worth it. Resilient individuals are better equipped to deal with the uncertainties and challenges of life, and can emerge stronger and more confident in the face of adversity. It is never too late to start building resilience, and with time and effort, we can all develop the resilience we need to thrive in an ever-changing world.

Chapter 14: Flexibility and Adaptability

- Importance of being flexible and adaptive in a changing world

In today's rapidly changing world, the importance of being flexible and adaptive cannot be understated. With technological advancements, shifting market trends, and global crises such as the COVID-19 pandemic, individuals and organizations alike must be prepared to pivot and adjust their strategies in order to thrive in an ever-evolving landscape. Being flexible and adaptive allows us to embrace change, overcome obstacles, and seize new opportunities that may arise.

One of the key benefits of being flexible and adaptive is the ability to respond quickly to changes in the environment. In today's fast-paced world, trends and situations can shift rapidly, and those who are able to adapt and adjust their plans accordingly are more likely to succeed. For example, during the COVID-19 pandemic, businesses that were able to quickly shift their operations online or pivot to producing essential goods were better positioned to weather the storm than those that were unable to adapt.

In addition to responding quickly to external changes, being flexible and adaptive also allows individuals and organizations to embrace innovation and creativity. By being open to new ideas and ways of doing things, we can discover fresh approaches to problem-solving and discover new opportunities for growth. This mindset of flexibility and adaptability fosters a culture of experimentation and continuous improvement, leading to better outcomes in the long run.

Furthermore, being flexible and adaptive can help individuals and organizations build resilience in the face of adversity. In times of crisis or uncertainty, those who are able to adapt and find solutions to unexpected challenges are more likely to bounce back and thrive in the aftermath. By developing a mindset of flexibility and adaptability, we can build the skills and strategies necessary to navigate difficult situations and emerge stronger on the other side.

Lastly, being flexible and adaptive is essential for personal and professional growth. In today's rapidly changing world, lifelong learning and skill development are crucial for staying competitive and relevant in the workforce. By being open to new experiences, willing to learn from failure, and adaptable to change, we can continue to evolve and grow as individuals. This willingness to embrace change and challenge ourselves can lead to new opportunities, experiences, and achievements that may not have been possible otherwise. By embracing change, responding quickly to external shifts, fostering innovation and creativity, building resilience, and committing to personal and professional growth, individuals and organizations can thrive in today's rapidly evolving landscape. Developing a mindset of flexibility and adaptability is crucial for success in the modern world, and those who cultivate these skills will be well-positioned to navigate the challenges and seize the opportunities that lie ahead.

- Teaching children how to adjust to new situations

Adjusting to new situations can be a daunting task for children, as change can bring about feelings of uncertainty and anxiety. As educators, it is our responsibility to help children navigate these transitions and create a sense of security and stability in their lives. By teaching children how to adjust to new situations, we can empower them to face challenges with confidence and resilience.

One important aspect of helping children adjust to new situations is providing a supportive and nurturing environment. Children need to feel safe and secure in order to effectively cope with change. As teachers, we can create a sense of continuity and consistency in the classroom by establishing clear routines and expectations. By setting predictable schedules and creating a positive and welcoming atmosphere, we can help children feel more at ease and confident in their ability to adapt to new situations.

In addition to creating a supportive environment, it is also important to teach children valuable coping skills that will help them navigate change. One effective strategy is to teach children how to identify and express their emotions in a healthy way. By encouraging open communication and providing opportunities for children to talk about their feelings, we can help them develop emotional intelligence and build resilience in the face of new situations.

Another important skill to teach children is problem-solving. When faced with new situations, children may encounter obstacles and challenges that they are unsure how to navigate. By teaching children how to brainstorm solutions, evaluate options, and make informed decisions, we can empower them to overcome obstacles and adapt to change more effectively.

Furthermore, it is important to teach children the importance of adaptability and flexibility. Change is a constant in life, and the ability to adjust to new situations is a valuable skill that will serve children well in their personal and academic lives. By teaching children how to embrace change with a positive attitude and a willingness to learn and grow, we can help them build a resilient mindset that will serve them well in the face of new challenges. By creating a supportive environment, teaching valuable coping skills, and fostering adaptability and resilience, we can empower children to navigate change with confidence and grace. As educators, it is our duty to provide children with the tools and resources they need to thrive in an ever-changing world. By helping children build the skills and mindset necessary to adjust to new situations, we can help them reach their full potential and lead fulfilling and successful lives.

- Embracing challenges as opportunities for growth

Embracing challenges as opportunities for growth is a crucial mindset to adopt in both personal and professional settings. Challenges are inevitable in life, and how we respond to them can greatly impact our development and success. Instead of viewing challenges as setbacks or obstacles, we should approach them as opportunities to learn, grow, and improve ourselves. By reframing our perspective on challenges, we can cultivate resilience, creativity, and a growth mindset that will enable us to navigate difficulties with confidence and grace.

One of the key benefits of embracing challenges as opportunities for growth is the development of resilience. Resilience is the ability to bounce back from setbacks, adapt to change, and persevere in the face of adversity. When we face challenges head-on and actively seek solutions, we build our resilience muscle and cultivate the mental toughness needed to overcome future obstacles. By viewing challenges as opportunities to test and strengthen our resilience, we can develop the capacity to navigate uncertainty and setbacks with grace and composure.

Additionally, embracing challenges as opportunities for growth fosters creativity and innovation. When we encounter challenges, we are forced to think outside the box and come up with creative solutions to overcome them. This process of creative problem-solving can stimulate our creativity and push us to think in new and innovative ways. By embracing challenges as opportunities for growth, we can tap into our creative potential and uncover new ideas, strategies, and approaches that can propel us forward in our personal and professional endeavors.

Furthermore, adopting a growth mindset towards challenges can lead to personal and professional growth. A growth mindset is the belief that our abilities and intelligence can be developed through effort and perseverance. When we approach challenges with a growth mindset, we view them as opportunities to learn, improve, and develop new skills. This belief in our capacity for growth and learning empowers us to take on challenges with confidence and optimism, knowing that we have the ability to overcome obstacles and emerge stronger and more resilient on the other side. By reframing our perspective on challenges and viewing them as opportunities for resilience, creativity, and personal growth, we can cultivate the mental fortitude and optimism needed to navigate difficulties with grace and confidence. So, next time you encounter a challenge, remember that it is not a roadblock, but rather a stepping stone on your journey towards growth and success. Embrace the challenge, learn from it, and watch yourself grow in ways you never thought possible.

Chapter 15: Promoting a Growth Mindset

- The concept of a growth mindset and its impact on confidence

The concept of a growth mindset has garnered widespread attention in recent years due to its profound impact on individual confidence and success. Coined by psychologist Carol Dweck, a growth mindset refers to the belief that abilities and intelligence can be developed through dedication and hard work. This stands in stark contrast to a fixed mindset, which views talents and abilities as innate and unchangeable. Those with a growth mindset tend to embrace challenges, persevere in the face of setbacks, and see failure as an opportunity for growth.

One of the key ways in which a growth mindset impacts confidence is by fostering a sense of resilience and self-efficacy. When individuals believe that their skills and abilities can improve over time, they are more likely to approach challenges with a positive attitude and a willingness to learn from their mistakes. This can lead to increased confidence in their ability to overcome obstacles and achieve their goals. In contrast, those with a fixed mindset may view setbacks as evidence of their inherent limitations, leading to feelings of self-doubt and insecurity.

Additionally, a growth mindset can empower individuals to take ownership of their learning and personal development. By recognizing that their efforts and perseverance play a crucial role in their success, individuals with a growth mindset are more likely to seek out opportunities for growth and continually strive to improve themselves. This proactive approach to self-improvement can boost confidence levels as individuals see tangible progress and accomplishments resulting from their hard work and dedication.

Furthermore, a growth mindset can help individuals cultivate a positive attitude towards failure. Instead of viewing setbacks as a reflection of their abilities or worth, those with a growth mindset see them as valuable learning experiences that can lead to growth and development. This mindset shift can prevent feelings of inadequacy and self-doubt from taking hold and instead foster a sense of resilience and perseverance in the face of adversity. As a result, individuals are more likely to approach challenges with confidence and a determination to succeed.

It is important to note that developing a growth mindset is not a one-time event but rather an ongoing process that requires effort and dedication. Individuals must actively challenge their fixed beliefs and work to cultivate a more adaptive and growth-oriented mindset. This may involve seeking out feedback, setting challenging goals, and reframing negative self-talk to focus on opportunities for growth and improvement. By consistently practicing these strategies, individuals can gradually shift their mindset towards one that is more aligned with a growth mindset and reap the benefits of increased confidence and self-belief. By embracing challenges, seeking out opportunities for growth, and reframing setbacks as learning experiences, individuals can cultivate a mindset that empowers them to overcome obstacles and achieve their goals. Through dedicated effort and a commitment to personal growth, individuals can develop a growth mindset that not only boosts their confidence but also sets them on a path towards continued success and fulfillment.

- Strategies for fostering a growth mindset in children

Developing a growth mindset in children is essential for their overall success and well-being. A growth mindset is the belief that abilities and intelligence can be developed through effort, perseverance, and learning from mistakes. This mindset fosters resilience, motivation, and a willingness to take on challenges. It is important for parents, educators, and caregivers to actively promote and reinforce a growth mindset in children from a young age. By doing so, we can empower children to reach their full potential and thrive in all areas of their lives.

One effective strategy for fostering a growth mindset in children is to praise their effort and hard work, rather than focusing solely on their intelligence or talent. When children are praised for their efforts, they learn that success is the result of hard work and dedication. This encourages them to persevere through challenges and setbacks, rather than giving up when faced with difficulty. By emphasizing the process of learning and growth, rather than just the end result, we can help children develop a growth mindset and a positive attitude towards learning.

Another important strategy for fostering a growth mindset in children is to teach them about the brain and how it can change and grow over time. When children understand that their brains are capable of growing and developing through practice and effort, they are more likely to embrace challenges and view mistakes as opportunities for learning and growth. By teaching children about the concept of neuroplasticity, we can help them adopt a growth mindset and develop a sense of agency over their own learning and development.

It is also crucial to create a supportive and nurturing environment for children to foster a growth mindset. Children thrive when they feel safe, valued, and supported in their learning and development. By providing encouragement, feedback, and guidance, we can help children build confidence in their abilities and develop a positive attitude towards learning. Creating a culture of growth and continuous improvement within the home or classroom setting can empower children to take risks, try new things, and push themselves beyond their comfort zones.

Additionally, setting realistic goals and expectations for children can help them develop a growth mindset and build resilience in the face of challenges. By breaking down larger goals into smaller, achievable steps, we can help children see progress and success along the way. This not only boosts their confidence and motivation, but also teaches them the importance of persistence and perseverance in achieving their goals. By modeling a growth mindset and demonstrating resilience in our own lives, we can inspire children to do the same and cultivate a positive outlook on learning and personal development. By praising their efforts, teaching them about the brain's ability to change and grow, creating a supportive environment, and setting realistic goals, we can empower children to embrace challenges, learn from mistakes, and strive for continuous improvement. It is important for parents, educators, and caregivers to actively promote and reinforce a growth mindset in children, as it lays the foundation for a lifelong love of learning and a positive outlook on personal development. By cultivating a growth mindset in children, we can help them reach their full potential and thrive in all areas of their lives.

- Teaching children to embrace challenges and setbacks

Teaching children to embrace challenges and setbacks is a crucial aspect of their overall development and growth. In today's fast-paced and competitive world, it is essential for children to learn how to navigate challenges and setbacks with resilience and perseverance. By teaching children these important skills from a young age, we can help them build the confidence and resilience they need to succeed in both their academic and personal lives.

One of the key ways to teach children to embrace challenges and setbacks is to encourage a growth mindset. A growth mindset is the belief that abilities and intelligence can be developed through hard work, perseverance, and dedication. By fostering a growth mindset in children, we can help them understand that setbacks and challenges are opportunities for growth and learning, rather than obstacles to be avoided. Encouraging children to see challenges as learning opportunities can help them develop a positive attitude towards setbacks and a willingness to persevere in the face of difficulties.

Another important aspect of teaching children to embrace challenges and setbacks is to provide them with the necessary support and guidance. Children need a supportive and nurturing environment in which they feel safe to take risks and make mistakes. By providing children with the support they need to navigate challenges and setbacks, we can help them develop the confidence and resilience to overcome obstacles and achieve their goals. Teachers, parents, and other caregivers play a crucial role in providing children with the encouragement and guidance they need to face challenges head-on.

It is also important to teach children the value of perseverance and hard work. In today's society, instant gratification is often prioritized over hard work and perseverance. However, by teaching children the importance of perseverance and dedication, we can help them develop the inner strength and determination they need to overcome challenges and setbacks. By instilling in children the value of hard work and perseverance, we can help them build the resilience and grit they need to navigate the ups and downs of life.

In addition to teaching children the value of perseverance and hard work, it is important to help them develop problem-solving skills. Encouraging children to think critically and creatively about challenges can help them develop the confidence and skills they need to overcome setbacks. By teaching children how to approach problems with a positive and open mindset, we can help them develop the resilience and adaptability they need to navigate challenges effectively. Problem-solving skills are essential for success in both academic and personal settings, and teaching children these important skills can help them thrive in a variety of situations.

Furthermore, it is important to teach children the importance of self-reflection and self-awareness. By helping children develop a greater understanding of themselves and their strengths and weaknesses, we can empower them to face challenges with greater confidence and resilience. Encouraging children to reflect on their experiences and learn from their mistakes can help them develop the self-awareness and emotional intelligence they need to overcome setbacks and grow from their experiences. By fostering a sense of self-awareness in children, we can help them develop the resilience and adaptability they need to navigate challenges effectively. By fostering a growth mindset, providing necessary support and guidance, teaching the value of perseverance and hard work, developing problem-solving skills, and encouraging self-reflection and self-awareness, we can help children build the confidence and resilience they need to succeed in both their academic and personal lives. By instilling in children the skills and mindset necessary to navigate challenges effectively, we can empower them to overcome obstacles and achieve their goals.

Chapter 16: Celebrating Diversity

- The importance of inclusivity and diversity in building confidence

Diversity and inclusivity are crucial aspects of building confidence in any workplace or community. By embracing diversity, we can create an environment where individuals from all backgrounds feel valued, respected, and empowered to contribute their unique perspectives and talents. This not only fosters a sense of belonging and acceptance, but also encourages collaboration, creativity, and innovation. Inclusivity ensures that everyone has the opportunity to thrive and succeed, regardless of their race, gender, ethnicity, sexual orientation, or any other characteristic. When individuals feel included and supported, they are more likely to have confidence in themselves and their abilities, leading to increased productivity, job satisfaction, and overall success.

One of the key benefits of diversity and inclusivity is the promotion of a growth mindset. When individuals are exposed to different perspectives and experiences, they are encouraged to think outside the box, challenge their own assumptions, and learn from others who may have different ways of approaching problems or tasks. This can help individuals develop a more open-minded and flexible attitude towards change and adversity, which is essential for building confidence in the face of challenges. In a diverse and inclusive environment, individuals are more likely to see setbacks as opportunities for growth and learning, rather than as failures. This can lead to increased resilience and self-efficacy, which are key components of confidence.

Inclusivity also plays a crucial role in combating stereotypes and biases that can undermine confidence and self-esteem. When individuals are treated with respect and fairness, regardless of their background, they are more likely to feel confident in their own abilities and worth. By breaking down barriers and promoting equality, inclusivity can help individuals overcome self-doubt and insecurity that may be perpetuated by societal norms or expectations. This can lead to a more positive self-image and sense of self-worth, which are essential for building confidence both personally and professionally.

Furthermore, diversity and inclusivity can contribute to a more inclusive and equitable society where everyone has the opportunity to succeed. By promoting diversity in leadership positions and decision-making processes, organizations can ensure that a wide range of perspectives are taken into account when making important decisions that affect the entire community. This can help create a more just and inclusive society where everyone has equal access to opportunities and resources, regardless of their background. When individuals see themselves represented and empowered in positions of influence, they are more likely to have confidence in their own abilities and potential to succeed. By creating a welcoming and supportive environment where everyone feels valued and respected, we can foster a sense of belonging, acceptance, and empowerment that can lead to increased self-confidence and success. Promoting diversity and inclusivity not only benefits individuals personally, but also contributes to a more open-minded, creative, and equitable society where everyone has the opportunity to thrive. By embracing diversity and inclusivity, we can build a more confident and resilient community that values and celebrates the unique contributions of all its members.

- Promoting acceptance and understanding of differences

Promoting acceptance and understanding of differences is essential in today's diverse and interconnected world. As globalization continues to bring people from different backgrounds and cultures together, it is becoming increasingly important for individuals to be open-minded, respectful, and empathetic towards others who may be different from themselves. By fostering a culture of acceptance and understanding, we can create a more inclusive society where all individuals feel valued and respected for who they are.

One way to promote acceptance and understanding of differences is through education. Schools and educational institutions play a crucial role in shaping the attitudes and beliefs of young people, who are the future leaders of our society. By incorporating diversity and inclusion into the curriculum, educators can help students develop a greater appreciation for the uniqueness of others. This can be achieved through teaching about different cultures, religions, and perspectives, as well as encouraging dialogue and communication among students from diverse backgrounds. By creating a safe and inclusive learning environment, schools can cultivate a sense of empathy and compassion in students, leading to greater acceptance and understanding of differences.

Another important way to promote acceptance and understanding of differences is through community engagement. Communities play a vital role in shaping social norms and attitudes towards diversity. By organizing events, workshops, and discussions that celebrate diversity and promote inclusion, community leaders can foster a sense of unity and acceptance among residents. By bringing people from different backgrounds together in a supportive and welcoming environment, communities can break down barriers and stereotypes, leading to greater understanding and empathy towards others. This can help create a more cohesive and harmonious society where individuals feel accepted and valued for who they are.

In addition to education and community engagement, promoting acceptance and understanding of differences also requires individual effort. Each of us has a role to play in building a more inclusive and accepting society. This can be as simple as listening to others with an open mind, being respectful of different perspectives, and challenging our own biases and prejudices. By being willing to step outside of our comfort zones and engage with people who are different from ourselves, we can broaden our horizons and develop a greater sense of empathy and compassion towards others. By cultivating a mindset of acceptance and understanding, we can create a more welcoming and inclusive environment for all individuals.

Ultimately, promoting acceptance and understanding of differences is a collective effort that requires the collaboration of individuals, communities, and institutions. By working together to foster a culture of acceptance and inclusion, we can create a more harmonious and interconnected society where all individuals feel accepted and valued for who they are. This not only benefits individuals on a personal level, but also promotes social cohesion and unity, leading to a more peaceful and prosperous society for all. By embracing diversity and celebrating our differences, we can build a more compassionate and inclusive world for future generations.

- Encouraging children to celebrate diversity in themselves and others

Encouraging children to celebrate diversity in themselves and others is an important and necessary aspect of their development. Diversity encompasses a wide range of differences, including but not limited to race, ethnicity, culture, religion, gender, sexual orientation, abilities, and socioeconomic status. By celebrating diversity, children learn to appreciate and respect the unique characteristics that make each person special. This not only creates a more inclusive and harmonious society, but also promotes social awareness, empathy, and understanding among individuals from different backgrounds.

One of the first steps in encouraging children to celebrate diversity is to foster a positive self-image. Children need to learn to be confident in who they are and to embrace their own differences. This can be achieved through positive reinforcement, encouraging them to be proud of their heritage, culture, and individual talents. Parents, teachers, and caregivers play a crucial role in helping children develop a sense of self-worth and identity. By instilling a strong sense of self-esteem, children are better equipped to appreciate and accept others for who they are.

In order to promote diversity, it is essential to expose children to different cultures, traditions, and perspectives. This can be done through books, movies, music, and other forms of media that showcase the richness and variety of the world around them. By learning about different customs and beliefs, children can gain a better understanding of the complexities of human experience and develop a sense of empathy towards others. Schools and community organizations can also play a pivotal role in promoting diversity by organizing cultural events, workshops, and educational programs that celebrate the unique backgrounds and contributions of all individuals.

Teaching children to respect and value diversity also involves addressing prejudice and discrimination. Children are not born with biases; these are learned behaviors that can be unlearned through education and exposure to different perspectives. It is important for parents and educators to have open and honest conversations about issues of race, privilege, and stereotypes. By addressing these topics head-on, children can learn to challenge their own assumptions and develop a more inclusive and accepting mindset. Additionally, teaching children about historical injustices and the struggles of marginalized communities can help cultivate a sense of social justice and activism.

In addition to fostering a sense of pride in one's own identity and promoting understanding of different cultures, celebrating diversity also involves teaching children the importance of inclusivity and acceptance. Encouraging children to be open-minded and tolerant towards others who may be different from them is essential in building a more cohesive and harmonious society. By teaching children to value diversity, we can help create a world where everyone is accepted and respected for who they are, regardless of their background or beliefs. In doing so, we can foster a sense of unity and belonging that transcends differences and promotes a more compassionate and equitable world for all. By promoting self-acceptance, cultural awareness, and inclusivity, we can help children build a strong foundation for understanding and respecting the differences that make each person unique. Through education, dialogue, and positive role modeling, we can create a more inclusive and harmonious society where all individuals are valued and accepted for who they are. By instilling these values in children from a young age, we can help shape a future where diversity is celebrated and embraced, leading to a more just and equitable world for all.

Chapter 17: Developing Problem-Solving Skills

- Importance of teaching children how to solve problems independently

Teaching children how to solve problems independently is a crucial skill that goes beyond the classroom and into their daily lives. Developing problem-solving skills at a young age not only empowers children to navigate challenges in school but also equips them with the tools needed to face real-world problems as they grow older. By encouraging children to think critically and independently, we are fostering their ability to make sound decisions, manage uncertainty, and overcome obstacles with confidence.

One of the key benefits of teaching children how to solve problems independently is the development of their critical thinking skills. Critical thinking is the ability to analyze and evaluate information to make informed decisions. By encouraging children to think critically about problems and challenges they encounter, we are helping them develop a strong foundation for decision-making in the future. Critical thinking skills enable children to assess situations, identify potential solutions, and make reasoned judgments based on evidence and logic.

Furthermore, teaching children how to solve problems independently helps them build resilience and adaptability. When children are able to face and overcome challenges on their own, they develop a sense of self-confidence and self-reliance. This, in turn, fosters a growth mindset that encourages them to persevere in the face of adversity and view setbacks as opportunities for growth. By teaching children how to solve problems independently, we are instilling in them the resilience and adaptability needed to thrive in an ever-changing world.

In addition, teaching children how to solve problems independently nurtures their creativity and innovation. When children are given the freedom to explore different solutions to problems without intervention, they are able to tap into their imagination and think outside the box. This creative thinking not only helps children come up with innovative solutions to problems but also fosters a spirit of curiosity and exploration. By encouraging children to think creatively and independently, we are inspiring them to embrace new ideas, experiment with different approaches, and push the boundaries of what is possible.

Moreover, teaching children how to solve problems independently promotes a sense of responsibility and accountability. When children are empowered to take ownership of solving problems on their own, they learn to accept the consequences of their decisions and actions. This sense of responsibility not only instills in them a strong work ethic but also teaches them the importance of taking initiative and being proactive in addressing challenges. By teaching children how to solve problems independently, we are helping them develop a sense of accountability that will serve them well in school, in their careers, and in their personal lives.

Ultimately, teaching children how to solve problems independently is essential for their overall development and success. By fostering critical thinking, resilience, creativity, responsibility, and accountability, we are equipping children with the skills and mindset needed to thrive in the 21st century. As educators and parents, it is our responsibility to empower children to become confident problem-solvers who are capable of facing any challenge that comes their way. By teaching children how to solve problems independently, we are helping them build a foundation for lifelong learning and growth.

- Strategies for developing critical thinking and problem-solving skills

Critical thinking and problem-solving skills are essential in today's complex and rapidly changing world. These skills are not only important in academic settings but also in the workplace and in everyday life. Developing these skills requires practice and dedication, but there are several strategies that can help individuals improve their critical thinking and problem-solving abilities.

One of the key strategies for developing critical thinking skills is to ask questions and challenge assumptions. It is important to not simply accept information at face value but to take a closer look and think critically about the information presented. This can involve asking questions such as "How do we know this information is true. " or "What are the underlying assumptions behind this argument. " By asking these types of questions, individuals can begin to develop a more critical mindset and learn to evaluate information more effectively.

Another important strategy for developing critical thinking skills is to practice active listening. Active listening involves fully engaging with the speaker and trying to understand their perspective before formulating a response. This can help individuals to become more aware of their own biases and assumptions and to consider alternative viewpoints. By actively listening and asking clarifying questions, individuals can improve their ability to think critically and communicate effectively.

In addition to asking questions and practicing active listening, it is important to consider multiple perspectives when developing critical thinking skills. This can involve seeking out diverse sources of information and considering different viewpoints on a particular issue. By exposing oneself to a variety of perspectives, individuals can broaden their understanding of complex issues and develop a more nuanced and informed opinion. This can also help individuals to identify potential biases and assumptions in their own thinking and to challenge them more effectively.

Problem-solving skills are closely related to critical thinking skills, as they involve the ability to analyze information, identify key issues, and develop effective solutions. One strategy for developing problem-solving skills is to break down complex problems into smaller, more manageable parts. By breaking a problem down into its component parts, individuals can better understand the underlying issues and develop a systematic approach to finding a solution. This can help to prevent individuals from feeling overwhelmed by complex problems and can make the problem-solving process more manageable.

Another important strategy for developing problem-solving skills is to practice brainstorming and creative thinking. This involves generating multiple potential solutions to a problem, even if some of them may seem unconventional or unlikely. By thinking creatively and considering a wide range of possible solutions, individuals can increase their chances of finding an effective solution to a problem. Brainstorming can also help individuals to think outside the box and to consider innovative approaches to problem-solving.

Collaboration is another key strategy for developing problem-solving skills. Working with others to solve problems can help individuals to consider different viewpoints and to benefit from the expertise and experience of others. By collaborating with colleagues, friends, or classmates, individuals can gain new insights into a problem and develop more effective solutions. Collaboration can also help individuals to practice communication and teamwork skills, which are essential in many professional settings. By asking questions, practicing active listening, considering multiple perspectives, breaking down complex problems, brainstorming creative solutions, and collaborating with others, individuals can improve their ability to think critically and solve problems effectively. These skills are not only important in academic and professional settings but also in everyday life, and can help individuals to navigate the challenges of an increasingly complex and interconnected world. By consistently practicing these strategies, individuals can continue to develop and strengthen their critical thinking and problem-solving skills over time.

- Encouraging creative and resourceful thinking

Encouraging creative and resourceful thinking is imperative in today's fast-paced and ever-changing world. In order to thrive in an increasingly competitive and complex environment, individuals must be able to think outside the box and come up with innovative solutions to challenges and problems. Creativity and resourcefulness are not only valuable skills in the workplace, but they are also crucial for personal growth and development. By cultivating these skills, individuals can enhance their problem-solving abilities, boost their confidence, and improve their overall quality of life.

To encourage creative and resourceful thinking, it is important to create an environment that fosters innovation and experimentation. This can be achieved by providing opportunities for individuals to explore new ideas, take risks, and think critically about the world around them. Additionally, it is essential to promote a culture of collaboration and diversity, where individuals are encouraged to share their unique perspectives and work together to solve problems. By fostering a sense of community and openness, individuals can feel more comfortable expressing their creativity and tapping into their potential.

One effective way to encourage creative and resourceful thinking is to provide individuals with the tools and resources they need to succeed. This can include access to training and development programs, workshops, and mentorship opportunities that can help individuals hone their creative skills and learn new techniques for problem-solving. Additionally, providing individuals with the freedom to explore their interests and passions can also inspire creativity and innovation. By allowing individuals to pursue their own projects and ideas, they can tap into their potential and discover new ways of thinking.

Furthermore, it is important to recognize and reward individuals for their creative and resourceful thinking. By acknowledging and celebrating their accomplishments, individuals are more likely to continue to think outside the box and come up with innovative solutions. This can be done through formal recognition programs, awards, or simply by providing positive feedback and encouragement. By highlighting the value of creativity and resourcefulness, individuals are more likely to embrace these skills and apply them in their daily lives. By creating a supportive environment, providing individuals with the tools they need to succeed, and recognizing and rewarding their achievements, we can cultivate a culture of innovation and creativity that will benefit individuals and society as a whole. By fostering creativity and resourcefulness, we can empower individuals to reach their full potential and make a positive impact on the world around them.

Chapter 18: Setting Boundaries and Consistency

- The role of boundaries in promoting confidence and self-esteem

Boundaries play a crucial role in promoting confidence and self-esteem in individuals. By defining and asserting boundaries, individuals establish a sense of control over their own lives and interactions with others. Boundaries serve as guidelines for determining what is acceptable and unacceptable behavior in relationships, both personal and professional. When individuals are able to set and maintain boundaries, they demonstrate self-respect and self-worth, which in turn fosters a positive sense of self-esteem.

One of the key ways in which boundaries promote confidence and self-esteem is by helping individuals establish a clear sense of identity. When individuals are able to define their own values, beliefs, and needs, they are better equipped to communicate these to others and establish healthy relationships. By setting boundaries, individuals signal to others what they are willing to tolerate and what is unacceptable to them. This clarity in communication not only helps individuals assert themselves but also fosters a sense of self-respect and self-worth.

Additionally, boundaries serve as a form of self-care and self-protection. By setting boundaries, individuals prioritize their own well-being and mental health. Boundaries help individuals establish limits on their time, energy, and emotions, preventing them from being taken advantage of or becoming overwhelmed. When individuals respect their own boundaries, they send a message to others that they are deserving of respect and consideration. This validation of one's own needs and boundaries can have a positive impact on self-esteem, as individuals feel empowered and in control of their own lives.

Furthermore, boundaries help individuals establish a sense of autonomy and agency. When individuals are able to assert their boundaries and make choices that align with their values and beliefs, they develop a sense of agency over their own lives. This sense of autonomy can lead to increased self-confidence and self-esteem, as individuals feel more in control of their own destiny. By respecting their own boundaries and asserting their needs and desires, individuals demonstrate to themselves and others that they are capable and deserving of respect.

In addition to promoting confidence and self-esteem, boundaries also play a crucial role in maintaining healthy relationships. By setting and maintaining boundaries, individuals establish clear expectations for how they wish to be treated by others. This clarity in communication helps prevent misunderstandings and conflicts, as individuals are better able to express their needs and boundaries. When individuals set and enforce boundaries in their relationships, they create a sense of mutual respect and understanding that is essential for building strong and healthy connections with others.

It is important to note that setting boundaries is not always easy, especially for individuals who may have a history of people-pleasing or codependent behaviors. However, learning to establish boundaries is a valuable skill that can be developed over time with practice and self-reflection. By recognizing their own needs and values, individuals can begin to assert their boundaries in a confident and assertive manner. Seeking support from a therapist or counselor can also be helpful in navigating boundary-setting and establishing healthy relationships. By setting and maintaining boundaries, individuals establish a sense of control over their own lives and interactions with others. Boundaries help individuals define their identity, prioritize their well-being, and establish agency and autonomy. By respecting their own boundaries and communicating their needs to others, individuals can build healthy relationships based on mutual respect and understanding. Developing the ability to set boundaries is an important step towards cultivating self-esteem and confidence in one's own worth and value.

- Strategies for setting and enforcing boundaries effectively

Setting and enforcing boundaries is a crucial aspect of maintaining healthy relationships, both in personal and professional settings. Boundaries are the limits we set for ourselves in order to protect our physical, emotional, and mental well-being. Without clear boundaries, we can easily become overwhelmed, resentful, or taken advantage of. In order to set and enforce boundaries effectively, it is important to have a clear understanding of what our needs and limits are, as well as the tools and strategies to communicate them assertively and respectfully.

One key strategy for setting boundaries effectively is to first identify and clarify your own needs and limits. This requires self-awareness and introspection to understand what is important to you and what you are willing to tolerate. Take some time to reflect on your values, beliefs, and priorities in order to determine what boundaries are necessary for you to feel safe and respected in your relationships. Consider what behaviors or actions from others cross the line for you and make you feel uncomfortable or violated. By having a clear understanding of your own boundaries, you will be better equipped to communicate them to others.

Once you have identified your boundaries, the next step is to communicate them assertively and respectfully to others. This can be challenging, especially if you are not used to advocating for your own needs. It is important to remember that setting boundaries is not selfish or rude, but rather a sign of self-respect and self-care. When communicating your boundaries, be direct and specific about what you need and why it is important to you. Use "I" statements to express your feelings and avoid blaming or accusing others. For example, instead of saying "You always make me feel ignored," you could say "I feel hurt when you don't listen to me. "

In addition to verbal communication, it is also important to set boundaries through your actions and behaviors. This means being consistent in enforcing your boundaries and not allowing others to disrespect them. If someone repeatedly crosses your boundaries, it is important to follow through with consequences in order to show that you are serious about maintaining them. This can be challenging, especially if you are accustomed to avoiding conflict or prioritizing others' needs over your own, but it is essential in order to establish healthy and respectful relationships.

Another important strategy for setting and enforcing boundaries effectively is to practice self-care and self-compassion. Setting boundaries can be emotionally draining and may result in conflict or pushback from others. It is important to take care of yourself and engage in activities that help you relax and recharge. This could include exercise, meditation, hobbies, or spending time with loved ones. Remember that setting boundaries is a form of self-love and self-respect, and it is important to treat yourself with kindness and compassion as you navigate this process.

It is also important to be open to feedback and willing to adjust your boundaries as needed. Our boundaries may change over time as we grow and evolve, and it is important to be flexible and adaptive in our relationships. If someone expresses discomfort or dissatisfaction with a boundary you have set, take the time to listen and understand their perspective. You may need to reevaluate your boundaries and make adjustments in order to find a compromise that respects both your needs and the needs of others. By identifying your own needs and limits, communicating them assertively and respectfully, and enforcing them through your actions, you can establish clear and non-negotiable boundaries that protect your well-being and foster mutual respect with others. Remember that setting boundaries is not selfish or rude, but rather a sign of self-respect and self-care. Practice self-compassion and be open to feedback as you navigate the process of setting and enforcing boundaries in your relationships.

- Importance of consistency in parenting practices

Consistency in parenting practices is a fundamental aspect of raising children that cannot be understated. It plays a pivotal role in shaping the behavior, development, and emotional well-being of children. Consistency refers to the predictability and reliability of a parent's actions, responses, and rules in their interactions with their children. When parents are consistent in their parenting practices, children are able to better understand boundaries, expectations, and consequences, which in turn helps to create a secure and stable environment for them to grow and thrive.

Consistency in parenting practices helps to establish a sense of structure and routine in the child's life, which is essential for their overall development. When parents consistently enforce rules and boundaries, children learn to understand what is expected of them and how to navigate different situations. This consistency provides children with a sense of security and predictability, which can help to reduce anxiety and uncertainty in their lives. Children thrive on routine and structure, and consistent parenting practices help to create a stable and supportive environment for them to thrive in.

Consistency in parenting practices also helps to build trust and strong relationships between parents and children. When parents are consistent in their responses and actions, children learn to trust that their parents will always be there for them and will provide them with the support and guidance they need. This trust forms the foundation for strong parent-child relationships, which are crucial for healthy emotional development and overall well-being. Consistent parenting practices help to foster open communication, mutual respect, and a strong sense of connection between parents and children.

Furthermore, consistency in parenting practices helps to teach children important life skills and values. When parents consistently reinforce positive behaviors and values, such as honesty, respect, and responsibility, children learn to internalize these values and apply them in their own lives. Consistent parenting practices also help children to develop self-discipline, self-control, and problem-solving skills, as they learn to navigate the consequences of their actions in a consistent and predictable manner. By modeling and reinforcing these important life skills and values, parents help children to develop into responsible, compassionate, and well-adjusted individuals.

In addition, consistency in parenting practices is crucial for shaping children's behavior and setting clear expectations. When parents are consistent in their responses to their children's behavior, children learn to understand the consequences of their actions and how to regulate their behavior accordingly. Consistency helps to prevent confusion and mixed messages, which can lead to behavioral issues and conflicts within the family. When parents establish consistent rules, consequences, and rewards, children learn to internalize these expectations and adjust their behavior accordingly. Consistency in parenting practices helps to create a harmonious and peaceful family environment where children feel safe, respected, and valued.

It is important to note that consistency in parenting practices does not mean being rigid or inflexible. Consistency is about being predictable, reliable, and fair in one's interactions with children, while also being responsive and adaptable to their individual needs and circumstances. Flexibility is an important aspect of effective parenting, as it allows parents to adjust their strategies and approaches based on the unique needs and personalities of their children. Consistency should be balanced with warmth, empathy, and understanding, as children need to feel loved, supported, and accepted by their parents. By finding a balance between consistency and flexibility, parents can create a nurturing and supportive environment that promotes the healthy development and well-being of their children. Consistency helps to create a stable and predictable environment for children to thrive in, while also fostering trust, strong relationships, and important life skills. By being consistent in their responses, actions, and values, parents can provide their children with the support, guidance, and structure they need to navigate the challenges of childhood and adolescence. Consistency is a key ingredient in effective parenting, and it is important for parents to strive for a balance between consistency and flexibility in their interactions with their children. By prioritizing consistency in their parenting practices, parents can help to nurture their children's growth, development, and overall well-being.

Chapter 19: Encouraging Independence and Resilience

- Steps to promote independence and self-reliance in children

As parents, caregivers, and educators, it is our responsibility to help children grow into self-sufficient and confident individuals. There are several steps that can be taken to foster independence in children from a young age.

One of the first steps in promoting independence in children is to give them opportunities to make choices and decisions on their own. Allowing children to make decisions, even small ones, helps them develop a sense of autonomy and self-confidence. For example, letting a child choose what to wear or what toy to play with can help them feel a sense of control over their own lives. As children get older, they can be given more freedom to make decisions about their daily activities, such as choosing extracurricular activities or planning their own schedule.

Another important step in promoting independence in children is to encourage them to take on age-appropriate responsibilities. By giving children tasks that they can handle, such as putting away their toys or making their bed, they learn valuable life skills and develop a sense of accountability. It is important to start small and gradually increase the level of responsibility as children grow older. This helps children build confidence in their abilities and prepares them for the responsibilities they will face as adults.

In addition to allowing children to make choices and take on responsibilities, it is important to encourage them to problem-solve and think critically. Teaching children how to think for themselves and find solutions to challenges helps them develop resilience and adaptability. Encouraging children to ask questions, explore different perspectives, and consider alternative solutions can help them become more independent and self-reliant. Parents and caregivers can support this process by providing guidance and support, but allowing children to take the lead in finding solutions to problems.

Furthermore, fostering independence in children involves teaching them important life skills that they will need as they grow older. This includes skills such as time management, organization, and communication. By teaching children how to manage their time effectively, keep track of their belongings, and express themselves clearly, we help them become more self-sufficient and confident in their abilities. Parents and caregivers can model these skills and provide opportunities for children to practice them in real-world situations.

Moreover, building independence in children also involves fostering a positive mindset and self-esteem. Children who believe in themselves and their abilities are more likely to take on challenges and succeed in reaching their goals. Encouraging children to have a growth mindset, where they see setbacks as opportunities for learning and growth, can help them develop resilience and persistence. Providing praise and encouragement for their efforts, rather than just their achievements, can also help children build confidence and self-esteem. By giving children opportunities to make choices, take on responsibilities, problem-solve, and develop important life skills, we help them become self-sufficient and confident individuals. By fostering a positive mindset and self-esteem, we empower children to navigate the challenges they will face in life with resilience and determination. As parents, caregivers, and educators, it is our duty to support and guide children on their journey toward independence and self-reliance.

- Teaching children to bounce back from setbacks

Teaching children to bounce back from setbacks is a crucial aspect of their development and growth. It is essential to equip children with the skills and resilience needed to navigate challenges and adversity in life. By instilling the importance of resilience at a young age, we can help children build a strong foundation for handling setbacks and overcoming obstacles in the future.

One of the key ways to teach children how to bounce back from setbacks is to foster a growth mindset. A growth mindset is the belief that abilities and intelligence can be developed through effort and perseverance. By encouraging children to approach challenges with a growth mindset, we can help them see setbacks as opportunities for learning and growth rather than as failures. This can help children develop a positive attitude towards challenges and setbacks, which will enable them to persevere in the face of adversity.

Another important aspect of teaching children to bounce back from setbacks is to help them develop problem-solving skills. Problem-solving skills are essential for overcoming obstacles and setbacks, as they allow children to come up with creative solutions to challenges they may face. By teaching children how to break down problems into smaller, more manageable tasks, we can help them develop the confidence and skills needed to overcome setbacks. This can help children develop a sense of agency and control over their lives, which can boost their resilience in the face of adversity.

In addition to fostering a growth mindset and problem-solving skills, it is important to teach children the importance of perseverance and resilience. Perseverance is the ability to keep going even when faced with obstacles and setbacks, while resilience is the ability to bounce back from adversity and setbacks. By teaching children how to persevere in the face of challenges and setbacks, we can help them develop the resilience needed to overcome obstacles and setbacks in the future. This can help children develop a sense of self-efficacy and confidence in their ability to overcome challenges, which can boost their resilience and ability to bounce back from setbacks.

It is also crucial to teach children the importance of self-care and self-compassion when it comes to bouncing back from setbacks. Self-care involves taking care of one's physical, emotional, and mental well-being, while self-compassion involves treating oneself with kindness and understanding in times of difficulty and hardship. By teaching children how to practice self-care and self-compassion, we can help them develop the emotional resilience and coping skills needed to bounce back from setbacks. This can help children develop a sense of self-awareness and self-acceptance, which can boost their confidence and resilience in the face of adversity. By fostering a growth mindset, problem-solving skills, perseverance, resilience, and self-care, we can help children develop the skills and resilience needed to navigate challenges and adversity in life. By equipping children with the tools and mindset needed to bounce back from setbacks, we can help them build a strong foundation for handling obstacles and setbacks in the future.

- Building resilience through challenges and adversity

Resilience is a crucial attribute that helps individuals navigate through life's challenges and adversities. It is the ability to adapt and bounce back from difficult situations, setbacks, and failures. Building resilience is a process that involves developing coping strategies, building social support networks, and cultivating a positive mindset. It is not about avoiding adversity or never experiencing difficulties but about learning how to effectively deal with them and grow stronger as a result.

One of the key ways to build resilience is through facing challenges head-on and embracing adversity as an opportunity for growth. When we avoid challenges or shy away from difficult situations, we miss out on important opportunities to learn and develop resilience. By stepping outside of our comfort zones and pushing ourselves to face challenges, we are able to build the mental and emotional muscles needed to bounce back from setbacks.

Another important aspect of building resilience is developing a support network of friends, family, mentors, and colleagues who can provide emotional support, advice, and encouragement during tough times. Research has shown that having a strong support system can significantly increase an individual's ability to cope with stress and adversity. By surrounding ourselves with people who believe in us and are willing to offer a listening ear or a helping hand when needed, we are better equipped to face challenges with confidence and resilience.

In addition to developing coping strategies and building a support network, cultivating a positive mindset is also essential for building resilience. Positivity and optimism can help us reframe challenges as opportunities for growth and learning, rather than insurmountable obstacles. By practicing gratitude, focusing on our strengths, and maintaining a sense of hope and optimism, we can better navigate through tough times and emerge stronger on the other side.

It is important to remember that building resilience is a lifelong journey that requires ongoing effort and commitment. It is not a one-time task that can be checked off a to-do list but a continuous process of growth and self-improvement. By embracing challenges, building a strong support network, and cultivating a positive mindset, we can develop the resilience needed to thrive in the face of adversity and emerge stronger and more resilient than ever before.

Ultimately, building resilience through challenges and adversity is about harnessing the power of resilience to overcome obstacles, grow as individuals, and thrive in the face of adversity. By developing coping strategies, building a support network, and cultivating a positive mindset, we can build the resilience needed to face life's challenges head-on and emerge stronger and more capable than ever before. So, embrace challenges as opportunities for growth, reach out for support when needed, and maintain a positive attitude as you navigate through life's ups and downs. Remember, resilience is not about avoiding adversity but about learning how to effectively deal with it and grow stronger in the process.

Chapter 20: Conclusion

- Recap of key concepts and strategies for building confident, happy kids

Building confident, happy kids is a crucial goal for parents, caregivers, and educators alike. Confident, happy children are more likely to succeed academically, socially, and emotionally. In order to help children grow into confident, happy individuals, there are several key concepts and strategies that can be implemented.

One important concept to understand when it comes to building confident, happy kids is the importance of positive reinforcement. Children thrive on praise and recognition for their efforts and achievements. By offering positive feedback and encouragement, parents and caregivers can help boost a child's self-esteem and confidence. This can be as simple as praising a child for completing a task or offering words of affirmation for a job well done.

In addition to positive reinforcement, setting realistic expectations is another key concept when it comes to building confident, happy kids. Children need to know that they are capable of achieving their goals and that their efforts will be rewarded. Setting achievable goals and celebrating small victories along the way can help children develop a sense of accomplishment and confidence in their abilities.

Another important strategy for building confident, happy kids is providing opportunities for them to develop their skills and talents. Encouraging children to participate in activities they enjoy and excel in can help boost their self-esteem and confidence. Whether it's sports, music, art, or academic pursuits, giving children the chance to explore their interests and talents can help them build a strong sense of self-worth and happiness.

Furthermore, fostering positive relationships and a supportive environment is essential for building confident, happy kids. Children thrive in environments where they feel loved, supported, and valued. By establishing strong relationships with children and creating a safe and nurturing environment, parents and caregivers can help children feel secure and confident in themselves.

Teaching children important life skills, such as problem-solving, communication, and resilience, is another key strategy for building confident, happy kids. Children who are equipped with these valuable skills are better able to navigate challenges and setbacks with confidence and resilience. By teaching children how to problem-solve and communicate effectively, parents and caregivers can help children develop the confidence and skills they need to succeed in all areas of their lives.

To summarize, it is important to remember that building confident, happy kids is an ongoing process that requires patience, consistency, and dedication. It is important for parents and caregivers to be supportive and encouraging, even when children face obstacles or setbacks. By providing a positive and nurturing environment, setting realistic expectations, and teaching important life skills, parents and caregivers can help children develop the confidence and happiness they need to thrive. Ultimately, building confident, happy kids is about helping children believe in themselves, develop their skills and talents, and cultivate positive relationships that support their growth and well-being.

- Final words of encouragement for parents on their parenting journey

Parenting is a challenging and rewarding journey that requires dedication, patience, and unconditional love. As parents, you play a crucial role in shaping the lives of your children and preparing them for the future. It is important to remember that you are not alone in this journey and that there is a community of support available to help you navigate the ups and downs of parenthood.

One of the most important things to remember as a parent is to be present and engaged in your child's life. Take the time to listen to their thoughts and feelings, and to participate in their interests and activities. Building a strong and loving relationship with your child is essential for their emotional and social development, and will help them feel supported and valued as they grow.

It is also important to set clear boundaries and expectations for your child, while also providing them with the freedom to explore and learn from their experiences. Encouraging independence and resilience in your child will help them develop the skills they need to navigate life's challenges and to become confident and capable individuals.

As you navigate the various stages of parenting, it is important to remember to take care of yourself as well. Parenting can be exhausting and overwhelming at times, and it is important to prioritize self-care and to seek support from family, friends, and professionals when needed. Remember that it is okay to ask for help, and that taking care of yourself will ultimately benefit your child as well.

Parenting is a journey filled with ups and downs, triumphs and challenges. But at the end of the day, remember to celebrate the small victories and cherish the precious moments with your child. Your love and support will shape their future and help them become the best version of themselves. Trust in your instincts, be patient with yourself and your child, and remember that you are doing an amazing job as a parent. Your dedication and love will make a lasting impact on your child's life, and will help them navigate the world with confidence and resilience. Remember, you are not alone in this journey, and there is a community of support available to help you every step of the way. Embrace the journey, cherish the moments, and know that you are making a difference in the life of your child.

- Looking ahead to a future of confident and self-assured children

Looking ahead to a future of confident and self-assured children is a topic of great importance in today's society. As parents, educators, and caregivers, it is essential that we work together to nurture and develop the self-esteem and confidence of our children. Research has shown that children who are confident and self-assured are more likely to succeed academically, socially, and emotionally. They are also better equipped to navigate the challenges and obstacles that they will inevitably face in their lives.

There are several key factors that contribute to the development of confidence and self-assurance in children. One of the most important is creating a supportive and nurturing environment in which children feel safe to express themselves and take risks. This means providing them with encouragement and positive reinforcement when they try new things, make mistakes, and learn from their experiences. It also means setting realistic expectations and goals for them, and offering guidance and support as they work towards achieving them.

Another key factor in building confident and self-assured children is fostering a sense of autonomy and independence. Children who are given the opportunity to make their own choices and decisions, and to take on age-appropriate responsibilities, develop a strong sense of self-efficacy and confidence in their abilities. This can be achieved by encouraging children to problem solve, think critically, and take initiative in their own learning and development.

Building strong relationships with children is also essential in helping them to develop confidence and self-assurance. Research has shown that children who have secure and positive relationships with their caregivers are more likely to have higher levels of self-esteem and self-confidence. This can be achieved by actively listening to children, showing empathy and understanding, and providing them with love, support, and affection. It is also important to model positive behavior and communication skills, as children learn by example.

In addition to creating a supportive and nurturing environment, it is important to help children develop a growth mindset. This means teaching them to view challenges and setbacks as opportunities for growth and learning, rather than as failures. By encouraging children to persevere, learn from their mistakes, and try new things, we can help them develop resilience, grit, and a positive attitude towards taking on new challenges.

It is crucial that we also teach children the value of self-care and self-compassion. In today's fast-paced and demanding world, children are often under pressure to excel academically, socially, and extracurricularly. This can lead to high levels of stress, anxiety, and self-doubt. By teaching children to prioritize their own well-being, practice self-care, and be kind to themselves, we can help them develop a strong sense of self-worth and confidence.

Looking ahead to a future of confident and self-assured children is not only important for their own well-being and success, but also for the well-being and success of society as a whole. Confident and self-assured children are more likely to become confident and self-assured adults, who are capable of making positive contributions to their communities and the world. By working together to nurture and develop the self-esteem and confidence of our children, we can help them reach their full potential and build a brighter future for all.